SALVATION

An In-Depth Study

ISBN: 13: 978-0692244586
ISBN: 10: 0692244581

Salvation, An In-Depth Study
Sheila R. Vitale

Living Epistles Ministries
Sheila R. Vitale
P O Box 562
Port Jefferson Station, NY 11776-0562

For My Parents
Louis and Evelyn Goldstein

Living Epistles Ministries

~ Judeo-Christian Spiritual Philosophy ~
Sheila R. Vitale
Pastor, Teacher, Founder
PO Box 562
Port Jefferson Station, NY 11776 USA

SALVATION
An In-Depth Study

**Edited and Adapted as a Book by
Sheila R. Vitale**

SALVATION

Is an Adaptation based on a Transcript of
LEM Message #24

Transcribed and Edited For
Clarity, Continuity of Thought, And Punctuation by
The LEM Transcribing and Editing Team

Formatted As a Book by
The LEM Professional Software Specialist Staff

Living Epistles Ministries
Sheila R. Vitale
Pastor, Teacher & Founder

Ministry Staff
Anthony Milton, Teacher (South Carolina)
Brooke Paige, Teacher (New York)
Sandra Aldrich (MN) (July 7, 1975 – April 18, 2021)

Administrative Staff
Susan Panebianco, Office Manager

Editorial Staff
Rose Herczeg, Editor

Technical Staff
Lape Mobolaji-Lawal, Database Administrator

Ministry Illustrators
Cecilia H. Bryant (Oct. 18, 1921 – Oct. 23, 2013)
Fidelis Onwubueke

Music Staff
June Eble, Singer, Lyricist and Clarinetist
(July 20, 1931 – Jan. 24, 2024)
Don Gervais, Singer, Lyricist and Guitarist
Rita L. Rora, Singer, Lyricist and Guitarist

TABLE OF CONTENTS

The Alternate Translation Bible©

***The Alternate Translation Bible* (ATB)**
Is an original interpretation of the Scripture.
It is not intended to replace traditional translations.

Alternate Translation of the Old Testament©
Alternate Translation, Exodus, Chapter 32
   (Crime of the Calf)©
Alternate Translation, Daniel, Chapter 8©
Alternate Translation, Daniel, Chapter 11©
Alternate Translation, Genesis 9:18-27
   (The Noah Chronicles, Second Edition) ©

Alternate Translation of the New Testament©
Alternate Translation, 2 Thessalonians, Chapter 2
   (Sophia)©
Alternate Translation, 1st John, Chapter 5©
Alternate Translation, the Book of Colossians
   (To The Church At Colosse) ©
Alternate Translation, the Book of Ephesians
   (To The Church At Ephesus) ©
Alternate Translation, the Book of Corinthians, Chapter 11
   (Corinthian Confusion) ©
Alternate Translation, the Book of Jude
   (The Common Salvation)©

Alternate Translation of the Book of the Revelation of
   Jesus Christ to St. John©
Traducción Alternada del Libro de Revelación de Jesucristo©

SALVATION

An In-Depth Study

WHO IS . . .

I. JESUS OF NAZARETH?

The Son of God

We are being created in stages, one man at a time. The many colors of the Spirit of God are layering over our soul to form Christ within us. Our soul is being saved; the Son of God is being born in us. We are waiting patiently for our bodies to be changed, and the end of the whole process is the glorification, or blending, of all of our parts into one, new spiritual man.

Jesus of Nazareth was the first man to bring the male offspring of God to term, and for this reason, he is called *the Son of God*.

Salvation is Son of God in the flesh, and his flesh came from the Jews.

Jehovah called out a small group of people and gave them his law. They served him for centuries, so by the time Jesus of Nazareth was born, there were a minimum of curses and evil spirits on that natural flesh line that God took as his own.

Every member of the soul that died is fallen, so it is quite a miracle that the Son of God was birthed in a human body. Christ, the Son of God, grew up with the soul man, Jesus, in Jesus' human body, and by the power of the resurrected Christ within himself, Jesus of Nazareth, purified his fallen soul.

Rom 1:4 – *Jesus, Son Of God*

> 4 AND **DECLARED TO BE THE SON OF GOD WITH POWER,** ACCORDING TO THE SPIRIT OF HOLINESS, BY THE RESURRECTION FROM THE DEAD: **KJV**

The Christ within Jesus of Nazareth was not corrupted by the soul that Jesus inherited from Mary. On the contrary, Jesus brought his fallen soul into submission to the Spirit of Holiness, and nailed it to Christ Jesus, the Son of God, within himself.

Gal 2:20 – *Crucified With Christ*

> 20 **I AM CRUCIFIED WITH CHRIST**: NEVERTHELESS I LIVE; YET NOT I, BUT CHRIST LIVETH IN ME: AND THE LIFE WHICH I NOW LIVE IN THE FLESH I LIVE BY THE FAITH OF THE SON OF GOD, WHO LOVED ME, AND GAVE HIMSELF FOR ME. **KJV**

The Spirit of Holiness declared Jesus to be the Son of God because Christ, the son of God, was dwelling within the man Jesus of Nazareth, and because Jesus' human soul was purified.

Mark's account of *the Temptation* says that Satan tested Jesus for forty days, and that Jesus overcame him.

Mark 1:13 – *Jesus Tempted*

> 13 AND HE WAS THERE **IN THE WILDERNESS FORTY DAYS, TEMPTED OF SATAN;** AND WAS WITH THE WILD BEASTS; AND THE ANGELS MINISTERED UNTO HIM. **KJV**

Jesus' soul and body came from Israelite DNA which was purified through Israel's obedience to Jehovah's Law of Ordinances.

Eph 2:15-16 - *Law Of Ordinances*

> 15 HAVING ABOLISHED IN HIS FLESH THE ENMITY, EVEN THE **LAW OF COMMANDMENTS CONTAINED IN**

ORDINANCES; FOR TO MAKE IN HIMSELF OF TWAIN ONE NEW MAN, SO MAKING PEACE;

16 AND THAT HE MIGHT RECONCILE BOTH UNTO GOD IN ONE BODY BY THE CROSS, HAVING SLAIN THE ENMITY THEREBY: **KJV**

The soul man is a three-fold creation. The Son of God lies on top of our human soul, and the Spirit of God lies on top of him. We started out as a soul man, and after that, God sent us the gift of the Holy Spirit from a higher spiritual world.

The waters rose up from under the earth when the flood came in Noah=s day, and water also came down from the heavens above. The anointing comes from Christ Jesus within us, and the Spirit of God comes from outside of us. The spiritual dew of God arises from within us, and the rain of God is poured out upon us.

The *Promise* comes from the heavens, layers over the soul man, and births Christ in humanity. Then, the Lord Jesus Christ, the third layer, arrives to shake the powers of the heavens and destroy Satan, the prince of this world.

John 12:31 – *Satan Cast Out*

31 NOW IS THE JUDGMENT OF THIS WORLD: NOW SHALL **THE PRINCE OF THIS WORLD BE CAST OUT.** **KJV**

A completed man is a three-fold twisted cord. He is a complete man, and the righteous counterpart of the Nephilim, the evil giants who seduced mankind:

Eccl 4:12 – *Three-Fold Cord*

12 AND IF ONE PREVAIL AGAINST HIM, TWO SHALL WITHSTAND HIM; AND **A THREEFOLD CORD IS NOT QUICKLY BROKEN.** **KJV**

Gen 6:4 - *Giants*

4 THERE WERE GIANTS IN THE EARTH IN THOSE DAYS; AND ALSO AFTER THAT, WHEN THE SONS OF GOD CAME IN UNTO THE DAUGHTERS OF MEN, AND THEY BARE CHILDREN TO THEM, THE SAME BECAME MIGHTY MEN WHICH WERE OF OLD, MEN OF RENOWN. **KJV**

Jehovah's Name

The Lord Jesus Christ is Jehovah=s Name.

Isa 43:7 – *Jehovah's Name*

7 EVEN **EVERY ONE THAT IS CALLED BY MY NAME: FOR I HAVE CREATED HIM FOR MY GLORY**, I HAVE FORMED HIM; YEA, I HAVE MADE HIM. **KJV**

The Lord Jesus Christ is the only foundation upon which Christ Jesus, the Son of God, can be built.

1 Cor 3:11 – *Only One Foundation*

11 FOR **THERE IS NO OTHER BASE FOR THE BUILDING BUT THAT WHICH HAS [ALREADY] BEEN PUT DOWN, WHICH IS JESUS CHRIST.** **BBE**

John 10:30 – *One God & His Name*

30 I AND MY FATHER ARE ONE. **KJV**

John 17:11 – *United With God*

11 AND NOW I AM NO MORE IN THE WORLD, BUT THESE ARE IN THE WORLD, AND I COME TO THEE. HOLY FATHER, KEEP THROUGH THINE OWN NAME THOSE WHOM THOU HAST GIVEN ME **THAT THEY MAY BE ONE, AS WE ARE.** **KJV**

The power of God without the nature of God, is evil.

2 Cor 11:14-15 – *Angel Of Light*

14 AND NO MARVEL; FOR **SATAN HIMSELF IS TRANSFORMED INTO AN ANGEL OF LIGHT.**

15 THEREFORE IT IS NO GREAT THING IF **HIS MINISTERS ALSO BE TRANSFORMED** AS THE MINISTERS OF RIGHTEOUSNESS; WHOSE END SHALL BE ACCORDING TO THEIR WORKS. **KJV**

Do not be upset over this truth. Just ask the Lord Jesus to impregnate you with Christ.

II. THE LORD JESUS CHRIST?

Salvation

Name in the Scripture typifies *nature*, so the Name, Jesus Christ, reveals the nature of Jehovah.

Acts 4:12 – *Salvation In Jesus' Name*

> 12 NEITHER IS THERE SALVATION IN ANY OTHER: FOR **THERE IS NONE OTHER NAME UNDER HEAVEN GIVEN AMONG MEN, WHEREBY WE MUST BE SAVED. KJV**

We are being saved from death and hell, which is this world system that mankind fell into after Adam, our original ancestor committed adultery and was rejected by Jehovah.

Salvation, then, is reunion with Jehovah.

Since the fall of mankind, no one of fallen Adam's descendants has been able to restore the life-giving relationship that Adam had with Jehovah, until Jesus.

To this very day, Jesus is the only man who is fully alive because of his unity with Jehovah, who is life itself.

So, salvation is now a possibility for everyone who accepts God's offer to have a relationship with Jesus, the one man who has been restored to a righteous and living relationship with Jehovah.

Wherefore, Salvation is only in Jesus' Name, or, through a relationship with Jesus, the only one who has been reunited with

Jehovah, the source of life. (See, also, ***Salvation Is Appearing Twice***.)

This Truth is often understood to mean that other religions are wrong, and that their followers need to be saved from hell. But God desires educated decisions, rather than conversions based upon fear. Souls are won in the arena of ideas, but truths such as Buddha and Shiva are not from the world above. They are joined to the underworld. ***The Lord Jesus Christ is the only Name that can defeat death and grant eternal life without sorrow***

There is spiritual truth in Buddhism, but spiritual truth, alone, or religion, cannot save souls. As a group, Buddhists are sexually moral. Some live in monasteries and lead sacrificial lives that they hope will bring an end to reincarnation, but Buddhist rejection of this world's wickedness does not produce eternal life. Eternal life is a man, and His Name is Jesus Christ.

1 Tim 6:14-16 – *True Immortality*

14 .... OUR LORD JESUS CHRIST:

15 ... WHO IS THE BLESSED AND ONLY POTENTATE, THE KING OF KINGS, AND LORD OF LORDS;

16 WHO ONLY HATH IMMORTALITY, DWELLING IN THE LIGHT WHICH NO MAN CAN APPROACH UNTO; WHOM NO MAN HATH SEEN, NOR CAN SEE: TO WHOM BE HONOUR AND POWER EVERLASTING. AMEN. **KJV**

There is only one way to be saved, and that is through a relationship with the Lord Jesus Christ. We receive eternal life through a spiritual union with Jesus, not through knowledge, works, or experience. The issue is not whose religion is right. The issue is spiritual truth. A man dies when he falls from the 20th floor, even if he believes himself to be immortal.

The moral aspects of Hinduism and Buddhism can be a buffer against spiritual wickedness in this present world. The problem is that eternal life cannot be acquired through Buddha or Shiva. Hinduism and Buddhism cannot produce the life of the ages. God loves all mankind, but Jesus, alone, possesses true immortality, and His Name is the only Name by which men can be saved.

<u>Acts 4:10-12</u> – *Salvation Only In Jesus' Name*

10 BE IT KNOWN UNTO YOU ALL, AND TO ALL THE PEOPLE OF ISRAEL, THAT BY THE NAME OF JESUS CHRIST OF NAZARETH, WHOM YE CRUCIFIED, WHOM GOD RAISED FROM THE DEAD, EVEN BY HIM DOTH THIS MAN STAND HERE BEFORE YOU WHOLE.

11 THIS IS THE STONE WHICH WAS SET AT NOUGHT OF YOU BUILDERS, WHICH IS BECOME THE HEAD OF THE CORNER.

12 **NEITHER IS THERE SALVATION IN ANY OTHER: FOR THERE IS NONE OTHER NAME UNDER HEAVEN GIVEN AMONG MEN, WHEREBY WE MUST BE SAVED. KJV**

A Glorified Man

A glorified man is a spiritual man who has permission from God to be the *higher soul*, or the *soul of the soul* of a physical man.

<u>John 13:31</u> – *Son Of Man Glorified*

31 THEREFORE, WHEN HE WAS GONE OUT, JESUS SAID, **NOW IS THE SON OF MAN GLORIFIED**, AND GOD IS GLORIFIED IN HIM. **KJV**

Jesus was *glorified* when his physical body was integrated with his soul, which was attached to his father, and he received a spiritual body.

III. CHRIST?

A Spark of God

Col 1:27 – *Christ, Our Hope*

> 27 TO WHOM GOD WOULD MAKE KNOWN WHAT IS THE RICHES OF THE GLORY OF THIS MYSTERY AMONG THE GENTILES; WHICH IS CHRIST IN YOU, **THE HOPE OF GLORY**. **KJV**

Christ is the spark of God within mortal man.

Christ is bound to Cain and overcome by the powers of the fallen soul that bind him.

The man, Jesus of Nazareth, was *the Christ, the anointed representative of God*, in the days of his flesh.

Christ is the power of God.

1 Cor 1:24 – *The Power Of God*

> 24 BUT UNTO THEM WHICH ARE CALLED, BOTH JEWS AND GREEKS, **CHRIST THE POWER OF GOD**, AND THE WISDOM OF GOD. **KJV**

Christ is the spiritual seed that carries the spiritual DNA, the nature (image) of God.

Gal 3:16 - *Christ*

> 16 NOW TO ABRAHAM AND HIS SEED WERE THE PROMISES MADE. HE SAITH NOT, AND TO SEEDS, AS OF MANY; BUT AS OF ONE, AND **TO THY SEED, WHICH IS CHRIST**. **KJV**

A Mystery

The mystery of Christ is that He:

Is the female seed that produces Christ Jesus, the spiritual male child that saves the personality,

Is an integral part of the process that saves the body, and,

Has the capacity to mature into Righteous Adam, the Son of God.

Christ is the heel of Righteous Adam, who is destined to bruise the seed of the Serpent.

The mystery of Christ's suffering, is that He lives on the inside of mankind, and is wounded by the sins of the people that He inhabits.

1 Cor 15:3-4 – *Christ Resurrected In Mankind*

> 3 FOR I DELIVERED UNTO YOU FIRST OF ALL THAT WHICH I ALSO RECEIVED, HOW THAT CHRIST DIED FOR OUR SINS ACCORDING TO THE SCRIPTURES;
>
> 4 AND THAT HE WAS BURIED, AND THAT HE ROSE AGAIN THE THIRD DAY ACCORDING TO THE SCRIPTURES: **KJV**

Jesus of Nazareth, the man, was *The Christ*, as opposed to *Christ, the female seed* that produces Righteous Adam.

The flesh body of Jesus of Nazareth was crucified and raised from the dead three 24-hour days later, because Christ, the female seed that died in a previous age, was already raised in the man, Jesus.

Rom 1:4 – *Christ Raised Previously*

4 AND [THAT THE SAME] SPIRIT OF HOLINESS THAT
DECLARED JESUS [TO BE] THE SON OF GOD, RAISED [HIM]
FROM THE DEAD, AND EMPOWERED [HIM TO BE] THE SUPREME
AUTHORITY OVER US. **KJV**

Today, the Lord Jesus Christ is delivering Christ, his female seed, through the Holy Spirit, and grafting his male seed, to Christ, his female seed, through the Doctrine of Christ.

Christ Jesus, the male offspring of the Lord Jesus Christ, has the power to raise mankind out of spiritual death.

2 Peter 3:15 – *Jesus Is Longsuffering*

15 AND ACCOUNT THAT <u>THE LONG SUFFERING OF OUR</u>
<u>LORD IS SALVATION</u>. **KJV**

The Lord Jesus Christ, suffered to learn obedience.

Language that, in the past, would have been heard only from sailors, is acceptable to many of our youth today, who sometimes even speak openly about their sexual escapades.

Christ suffered and continues to suffer today in the form of Christ Jesus, who lives inside of sinners. Christ is right in here with us when envy or lust rises up in our mind.

No one except Jesus has been totally delivered from lust, envy and pride, the foundational characteristics of the natural man.

Christ is inside of us, locked up within our flesh body. He lives with our sin nature every day, but he is faithful to stay with us, despite our ungodly thoughts. He suffers, but he stays, and the end of his faith in us, is the *salvation* of our soul. He is our only hope that we might be saved.

Abraham's Seed

Rom 12:5 – *One Body*

> 5 SO WE, BEING MANY, ARE **ONE BODY IN CHRIST**, AND EVERY ONE MEMBERS ONE OF ANOTHER. **KJV**

Christ is a many-membered, spiritual Body.

Rom 9:8 – *Children Of Promise*

> 8 THAT IS, THEY WHICH ARE THE CHILDREN OF THE FLESH, THESE ARE NOT THE CHILDREN OF GOD: BUT **THE CHILDREN OF THE PROMISE ARE COUNTED FOR THE SEED.** **KJV**

Wherever Christ dwells, he is always a part of the spiritual Body of Christ, and the man that Christ dwells in, is considered to be the physical offspring of Abraham, and an heir to the promises that Jehovah made to their father, but *the Holy Spirit is not Christ*.

Abraham's seed has the potential to produce a spiritual male child in a man, and that male child is called *the Son of God.*

The seed that Jehovah promised Abraham appeared in Abraham's son, Isaac. It is written, that the physical body of Messiah will come from Judah.

Gen 49:10 – *Judah, the Law Giver*

> 10 THE SCEPTRE SHALL NOT DEPART FROM JUDAH, NOR A LAWGIVER FROM BETWEEN HIS FEET, UNTIL SHILOH COME; AND UNTO HIM SHALL THE GATHERING OF THE PEOPLE BE. **KJV**

But the righteous spirit of Messiah's inner man, was always intended to be Elohim, the Spirit of God, the Creator, itself.

Gen 1:2 – *The Creator*

> 2 AND THE EARTH WAS WITHOUT FORM, AND VOID;
> AND DARKNESS WAS UPON THE FACE OF THE DEEP. AND **THE
> SPIRIT OF GOD MOVED UPON THE FACE OF THE WATERS.**
> **KJV**

And that Spirit, in seed form, was transferred from Jacob to his son, Joseph:

Gen 49:24 – *Joseph, The Righteous Seed*

> 24 BUT HIS BOW ABODE IN STRENGTH, AND THE ARMS
> OF HIS HANDS WERE MADE STRONG BY THE HANDS OF THE
> MIGHTY GOD OF JACOB; **(FROM THENCE IS THE SHEPHERD,
> THE STONE OF ISRAEL) KJV**

Joseph's righteous seed was delivered to Jesus through his spiritual father, the spirit of Elijah, a compound soul which includes an Egyptian ancestor who was an Ephrathite.

The Anointing

Isa 10:27 – *The Anointing Oil*

> 27 AND IT SHALL COME TO PASS IN THAT DAY,
> THAT HIS BURDEN SHALL BE TAKEN AWAY FROM OFF
> THY SHOULDER, AND HIS YOKE FROM OFF THY NECK,
> AND **THE YOKE SHALL BE DESTROYED BECAUSE OF
> THE ANOINTING. KJV**

The Hebrew word translated *Christ*, means *anointed*. *Christ Jesus* is the Son of God. He is the spiritual oil that rescues *Christ* from the grip of the principalities that rule this world.

Fully expressed, it means, *to consecrate someone as king*:

Salvation/ Christ?

<u>Rev 5:10</u> – *Kings & Priests*

> 10 AND HAST MADE US UNTO OUR GOD KINGS AND PRIESTS: AND WE SHALL REIGN ON THE EARTH. **KJV**

IV. THE MAN, CHRIST JESUS?

Savior

There are two Hebrew and three Greek words translated *Salvation*.

Tashua means, **national, spiritual** or **personal rescue.** *Tashua* is Jesus Christ, who abides, today, in the God world at the right hand of God.

Yashuah means, **something saved, that which is saved, delivered**. It also means, victory, **prosperity, health and welfare.** *Yashuah* is Christ Jesus, the Angel of Salvation in the midst of us.

Jewish Christians call Jesus *Yeshuwah HaMashia*. *Yeshuwah* is the word that means, *Salvation*, and that is of the soul, but *HaMashia* is a little different. The word, *Christ*, in the Hebrew is *Mashia*. *Ha* means *The*. *Yshuwah Hamashia* then means, *the Savior of my soul, my Christ*.

Gen 2:18 – *A Help Meet*

18 AND THE LORD GOD SAID, IT IS NOT GOOD THAT THE MAN SHOULD BE ALONE; **I WILL MAKE HIM AN HELP MEET FOR HIM. KJV**

There is a third Hebrew word that means, *Savior*, *the one who aids, or helps*. God promised Adam assistance, a help meet.

17

Eph 5:23 – *Savior Of The Body*

> 23 FOR THE HUSBAND IS THE HEAD OF THE WIFE,
> EVEN AS CHRIST IS THE HEAD OF THE CHURCH: AND HE IS **THE**
> **SAVIOUR OF THE BODY. KJV**

The definition of the word, *helpmeet*, is *an aid*. *Aid,* according to *Webster's Dictionary*, means *a wall*. The definition of *aid*, is a *wall* that joins with Adam to make him a wall and a defensed city.

This *Hebrew* word that means *Savior*, speaks about *Christ Jesus, the Son of Jesus Christ*, the *savior* in the midst of us.

The *Greek* word, translated, *salvation*, *Strong's #4991*, and the *Hebrew* word, *Yshuwah*, translated, *salvation*, are female. *Yasha, Savior,* is also female, but there is no gender attributed to the *Greek* word translated *Savior* by either *Strong* or *Gesenius.* Neither translator could explain why the *Greek* word, *Savior, meaning, Jesus,* would be female, so they both chose not to attribute either sex to the Greek word translated *Messiah*.

The Savior, Christ Jesus, is the man that S*alvation* inhabits, the man that stands in front of the Prince who is Salvation, the man that Salvation appears to the world through.

Jesus is the *Savior of our soul*. He saves us by joining the male seed of his perfected, glorified, soul to our sinful soul. But our sin will not contaminate Jesus= seed, which is his Son. On the contrary, Christ Jesus, Jesus' Son, will consume our sinful soul

Christ Jesus is the only Mediator between man and God.

1 Tim 2:5 - *Mediator*

> 5 FOR THERE IS ONE GOD, AND **ONE MEDIATOR**
> **BETWEEN GOD AND MEN**, THE MAN CHRIST JESUS; **KJV**

Overlaid With Gold

1 Kings 6:21 – *Overlaid with Gold*

> 21 SO SOLOMON OVERLAID THE HOUSE WITHIN WITH PURE GOLD: AND HE MADE A PARTITION BY THE CHAINS OF GOLD BEFORE THE ORACLE; AND HE **OVERLAID IT WITH GOLD**. **KJV**

The Tabernacle is the Old Testament type of the relationship between *Christ* and *Christ Jesus*. Wood typifies mortal man, and gold suggests deity.

Christ Jesus is overlaying *Christ* to preserve him, and to strengthen him to overcome the ungodly powers that have subjected him.

The Hebrew word translated *Christ*, is from a root that means *to draw the hand over something*. It means, especially, *to lay colors on something*.

To lay colors on something, also means, *to anoint with oil*. Fully expressed, it means, *to consecrate someone as king*:

The Hebrew word translated *Christ*, means, *anointed*. It is from a root that means *to draw the hand over something*. It means, especially, *to lay colors on something*.

Acts 10:38 – *Jesus Anointed*

> 38 HOW GOD **ANOINTED JESUS OF NAZARETH WITH THE HOLY GHOST AND WITH POWER**: WHO WENT ABOUT DOING GOOD, AND HEALING ALL THAT WERE OPPRESSED OF THE DEVIL; FOR GOD WAS WITH HIM. **KJV**

White Light And Colors

Bright, white light separates into the colors of the rainbow when it shines through a prism. Likewise, the Spirit of the invisible God is revealed when it shines through the prism of mankind.

The glorified Jesus Christ, who is now joined to the Spirit of God, is revealing himself through the spiritual red earth of mankind. *The glorified Jesus* is the bright, white, light, and *Christ Jesus, the Son*, is the spectrum of the rainbow, God's white light in its lower form. The Father is above, the Son is below.

Joseph's many-colored coat is a type of Christ Jesus, the representative of God in the earth. *The glorified Jesus Christ*, is laying *Christ Jesus*, his colors, on the soul man, so that he can be seen in this visible world.

The Immortality Of Innocence

Jude 6:6 – *First Estate*

> 6 AND **THE ANGELS WHICH KEPT NOT THEIR FIRST ESTATE**, BUT LEFT THEIR OWN HABITATION, HE HATH RESERVED IN EVERLASTING CHAINS UNDER DARKNESS UNTO THE JUDGMENT OF THE GREAT DAY. **KJV**

Christ Jesus, the Son, is the visible image of the invisible *Jesus Christ, his Father*. The fallen man that Christ Jesus is joined to when he reunites with the Lord Jesus, his Father above, shall be restored to righteous Adam=s first estate, which is the immortality of innocence.

Prophecy

Prophecy can come forth during a natural conversation, as well as from the floor of the Church. When Christ speaks through us, we are Christ. It is important that we develop our ability to recognize prophecy, and to pray for that ability if we do not have it. Without prophecy, we might not hear God when He speaks to us.

The Beginning

<u>*Rev 3:14*</u> – Beginning Of Creation

14 AND UNTO THE ANGEL OF THE CHURCH OF THE LAODICEANS WRITE; THESE THINGS SAITH THE AMEN, THE FAITHFUL AND TRUE WITNESS, **THE BEGINNING OF THE CREATION OF GOD**;   **KJV**

Christ Jesus, the Son of God in the flesh, is the creation of God.

WHAT DOES IT MEAN. . .

I. JESUS . . . .

Our Faith?

<u>Heb 12:2</u> – *Jesus, Our Faith*

> 2 LOOKING UNTO **JESUS THE AUTHOR AND FINISHER OF OUR FAITH;** WHO FOR THE JOY THAT WAS SET BEFORE HIM ENDURED THE CROSS, DESPISING THE SHAME, AND IS SET DOWN AT THE RIGHT HAND OF THE THRONE OF GOD. **KJV**

The natural man has *the hope of Salvation*, but true faith is only in Jesus Christ.

Jesus' Son is purifying the heart of fallen mankind, and the wickedness of our fallen soul cannot pollute him.

<u>Rom 12:21</u> –*Evil Overcome*

> 21 BE NOT OVERCOME OF EVIL, BUT OVERCOME EVIL WITH GOOD. **KJV**

<u>John 1:5</u> – *Light Illuminates*

> 5 AND THE LIGHT GOES ON SHINING IN THE DARK; IT IS NOT OVERCOME BY THE DARK. **BBE**

He suffered for us in the past, is still suffering for us, and will continue to suffer for us, until all of mankind has been brought into the image of his Son.

2 Tim 2:10 - *Salvation In Christ Jesus*

> 10 THEREFORE, I ENDURE ALL THINGS FOR THE ELECT'S SAKES, THAT THEY MAY ALSO OBTAIN **THE SALVATION, WHICH IS IN CHRIST JESUS** WITH ETERNAL GLORY. **KJV**

Not only did Jesus suffer for us, but Christ within many believers is suffering today, so that all mankind might enter into glory.

Have you been crucified lately? Has someone wronged you? Has someone hated you? Has someone betrayed you? Have you manifested Christ in response to those afflictions? Have you blessed your persecutors? Have you loved them? Have you responded out of your fallen soul, or have you responded out of Christ, the nature of God within you? Have you manifested righteousness to those who despise you? If you have, you are suffering with Christ so that they, too, might partake of the glory of God.

Jesus suffered, the apostles suffered, and we suffer and shall suffer, so that others can receive ***Salvation***. God does not require us to be victimized, but He will let us be crucified and expect us to bless the people who do it. But we have to use wisdom. We should stop someone from driving away in our brand-new car, but bless those who hurt us. Bless the woman who tries to steal your husband, but do not agree with what she is doing.

There is a difference between feeding and clothing the poor, and housing and supporting those who refuse to work. Set a time limit for the unemployed person to live in your home while they look for a job. Then, ask them to leave if they are not making an effort to find one. We can help them, bless them and pray for them, but they have to go to work.

2 Cor 1:5-7 - *Affliction*

5 AS THE SUFFERINGS OF CHRIST ABOUND IN US, SO OUR CONSOLATION ALSO ABOUNDS BY CHRIST.

6AND WHETHER WE BE AFFLICTED, **IT IS FOR YOUR CONSOLATION AND SALVATION**, WHICH IS EFFECTUAL, IN THE ENDURING OF THE SAME SUFFERINGS, WHICH WE ALSO SUFFER: OR WHETHER WE BE COMFORTED, **IT IS FOR YOUR CONSOLATION AND SALVATION.**

7AND OUR HOPE OF YOU IS STEADFAST KNOWING THAT AS YOU ARE PARTAKERS OF THE SUFFERINGS, SO SHALL YOU BE ALSO OF THE CONSOLATION. **KJV**

Sometimes we find ourselves in situations that cause ourselves and others to suffer. We suffer so that one or both of us might be consoled when Christ appears. We suffer unto the *salvation* of our soul. We suffer, they suffer, until the Comforter, who is the Spirit of Truth, comes.

John 15:26 – *The Comforter*

26 BUT WHEN **THE COMFORTER IS** COME, WHOM I WILL SEND UNTO YOU FROM THE FATHER, EVEN **THE SPIRIT OF TRUTH**, WHICH PROCEEDETH FROM THE FATHER, HE SHALL TESTIFY OF ME: **KJV**

God must be glorified, but sometimes, we do not see the victory for years.

There was a family of missionaries, for example, that was ministering on an Indian reservation, when a terrible incident occurred. The Indians were law abiding, but there was a criminal amongst them. He raped the missionary's thirteen-year-old daughter, and the child lost her mind.

The parents called all of the big-name evangelists for prayer. Everybody prayed, but the girl's mind was not restored. The other Indians were so horrified that one of their own would attack a missionary's daughter, that they reverted to their tribal law, and killed him.

After that, the Federal Government became involved (the Federal Government is responsible for crimes committed on Indian reservations), and institutionalized the girl, against the parents' wishes.

It is not clear whether or not the girl was violent, but the Government kept her in that mental institution until she was thirty-five years old. The missionaries continued to serve God until the girl's father died.

Sometimes we suffer so that the character of God should be developed in us. Sometimes God uses us to aid and assist others as we pursue our own *salvation*. Sometimes we have to be hurt to learn a few things. Sometimes we die to the flesh when people hurt us. Sometimes suffering matures us, and we become more like God in our thoughts and behavior. Sometimes dispensing the bread and the corn to the starving is not enough to change us. Sometimes it takes rejection and false accusation. Sometimes it takes going to jail.

Joseph was in Pharaoh's dungeon before he became the sole dispenser of corn during the Egyptian famine. His own brothers sold him into slavery, and then the wife of his master lied about him when he resisted her sexual advances. After that. Potiphar imprisoned Joseph in an Egyptian dungeon until God delivered him and exalted him before the whole world.

Sometimes we are so down that we cannot see our future in God, but we can always pray, ***Lord, let me see your purpose in my life. I know it exists, but I cannot see it. Help me to look beyond the trial and see the promise. Help me to survive this trial.*** He is faithful to help us.

There was a believer, once, who was so desperately sick that she thought she would lose her mind. She was too sick to leave the house, so she called everyone she could think of for help. Many believers prayed for her, but God did not move.

Finally, God spoke to her through a friend in Florida. She heard God's voice through her friend on her fifteenth call. Needless to say, by His grace and mercy she survived.

It is important to know how to function in the Spirit and to recognize God=s voice. If you do not have this ability, ask God for it. One day, your life may depend on it.

Our Redeemer?

1 Cor 6:17 - *One Spirit*

> 17 HE THAT IS JOINED TO THE LORD IS **ONE SPIRIT**
> KJV

Jesus purchased our human spirit. This means that all of the human spirits of mankind belong to Jesus, but he does not possess them all at this time. Jesus is in the process of joining his Spirit to the human spirits of mankind, by faith in His Name. Very little is required of the believer for his human spirit to be saved.

The preservation, or the salvation of our soul, is a different process. The human soul can also be called the human personality. The personalities of mankind are polluted from the spiritual filth of this world, but they can be cleansed by drawing near to Jesus through a knowledge of His Word.

1 John 5:19 - *Wickedness*

> 19 AND WE KNOW THAT WE ARE OF GOD, AND **THE WHOLE WORLD LIETH IN WICKEDNESS. KJV**

He will also, eventually, provide spiritual bodies for us. But, the processes of Salvation are not necessarily consecutive. Reconciliation, sanctification, preservation and redemption, do not always follow one after the other, in a specific order. On the contrary, everything works together simultaneously in the realm of the Spirit to produce one complete experience called *Salvation*.

Isa 28:12-13 – *True Rest*

12 TO WHOM HE SAID, THIS IS THE REST WHEREWITH YE MAY CAUSE THE WEARY TO REST; AND THIS IS THE REFRESHING: YET THEY WOULD NOT HEAR.

13 BUT THE WORD OF THE LORD WAS UNTO THEM **PRECEPT UPON PRECEPT, PRECEPT UPON PRECEPT; LINE UPON LINE, LINE UPON LINE**; HERE A LITTLE, AND THERE A LITTLE; THAT THEY MIGHT GO, AND FALL BACKWARD, AND BE BROKEN, AND SNARED, AND TAKEN. **KJV**

At first glance, the prophet appears to be instructing the people to learn the Scripture one line at a time. But he is actually mocking the religious establishment, whose traditions make the rest of God of no effect.

The last person into God's vineyard receives the same spiritual pay as the person that entered early in the morning.

You do not have to learn everything that your teacher learned nine years ago. You do not have to travel the route that he traveled. People sitting in a congregation can be advancing in God in half the time that it took their teacher.

Spiritual growth does not come from studying the Scripture line upon line, precept upon precept. God will teach you what He wants to teach you, when He wants to teach it to you. No one can put restrictions on God, not even the legalism of the Pharisees, and I mean the modern-day Pharisees.

God will tell you what He wants to tell you. This is how so many believers get messed up. They think that because they studied for fifteen years, someone with less time than they have, cannot possibly know more than they do.

They may be saved only six months, but you had better pray before you reject what they have to say. You better make sure that you are not talking to a prophet of God who came to you with a Word from God. It does not matter how old the person is. They do not even have to be human. God used an ass once. You had better try to discern the voice of the Lord, because your life may depend upon it.

Rev 14:2 – *God's Voice*

> 2 AND I HEARD **A VOICE FROM HEAVEN**, AS THE VOICE OF MANY WATERS, AND AS THE VOICE OF A GREAT THUNDER: AND I HEARD THE VOICE OF HARPERS HARPING WITH THEIR HARPS: **KJV**

Your God is the spirit that rules in you. There is more than one god. Jehovah never denied that there was more than one god. He just said that He is the God of gods. He said He is God Almighty.

Fallen Adam wants to be God. If you are following after the mind of fallen Adam that is in you, then he is your God, even if you speak in tongues and dance in the Spirit. When you walk out of that church, if you are doing what fallen Adam tells you to do, he is your God, at least for that moment.

Salvation to our God, which sitteth on the throne and unto the Lamb.

Rev 7:10 – *God's Throne*

> 10 AND CRIED WITH A LOUD VOICE, SAYING, SALVATION TO OUR **GOD WHICH SITTETH UPON THE THRONE**, AND UNTO THE LAMB. **KJV**

Christ Jesus is the Lamb of God.

We owe our *salvation* to Almighty God, who has joined Jesus= Spirit to our spirit, to purify it. Christ Jesus, the Son of God, can now sit on the throne of our heart, but he must be born in us first. There is no other way.

Our Rock?

Deut 32:15 – *Jesus, Our Rock*

15 But Jeshurun waxed fat, and kicked: thou art waxen fat, thou art grown thick, thou art covered with fatness; then he forsook God which made him, and lightly esteemed **the Rock of his salvation. KJV**

Rocks in the Scripture refer to spiritual power. Christ Jesus is our spiritual power. He is our defense against every spiritual power that is not of God. He is King of kings and Lord of lords, and his spiritual power can defeat any other spiritual power.

No matter how powerful Satan, the unconscious part of the carnal mind, is in our lives, the Lord Jesus Christ is full well able to defeat him.

The Bridegroom?

Jesus is appearing the second time to marry the man, Christ Jesus, in the people who accepted his first offer and received his seed.

Gal 3:16 – *Abraham's Seed*

16 Now to Abraham and his seed were the promises made. He saith not, And to seeds, as of many; but as of one, **and to thy seed, which is Christ. KJV**

Jesus carries Abraham's seed, which is Christ.

Heir of The World?

Rom 4:13 – Jesus, *Heir of The World*

13 For the promise, that he should be **the heir of the world**, was not to Abraham, or to his seed, through the law, but **through the righteousness of faith. KJV**

Jesus Christ has inherited the world and everything in it, which includes mankind. We belong to him.

Gal 3:29 – *Two Generations of Seed*

> 29 AND IF YE BE CHRIST'S, THEN ARE YE ABRAHAM'S SEED, AND HEIRS ACCORDING TO THE PROMISE. KJV

We are Abraham's seed when Christ, the Son of Jesus Christ, dwells in us.

Born Of A Woman?

Heb 9:28 – *Removal Of Sin*

> 28 CHRIST WAS ONCE OFFERED TO BEAR THE SINS OF MANY AND UNTO THEM THAT LOOK FOR HIM, SHALL HE APPEAR THE SECOND TIME, WITHOUT SIN UNTO SALVATION. KJV

Christ appeared for the first time in the man, Jesus of Nazareth. Jesus is the first man to experience complete salvation, spirit, soul and body. Jesus' physical body died and was converted into a spiritual body that was completely blended with his soul and spirit. Jesus died to his life in this world and became a glorified man.

Offered For Our Sins?

Jesus is planting the seed of Christ Jesus, the only mediator between God and man, in the spiritual universes of the physical men who receive him as savior.

Christ Jesus is the spiritual warrior that enables us to overcome our sin nature. The warfare between good and evil within the individual begins when Christ begins to appear.

God made one offer of **Salvation,** through faith in Jesus Christ, to the many members of humanity. That offer still stands and will continue to be available to the many, even after Jesus appears the second time.

A Ransom For Us?

<u>**1 Tim 2:5-6**</u> – *Christ Jesus, Our Ransom*

> **5** FOR THERE IS ONE GOD, AND ONE MEDIATOR BETWEEN GOD AND MEN, THE MAN CHRIST JESUS;
>
> **6** WHO GAVE HIMSELF *A RANSOM* FOR ALL, TO BE TESTIFIED IN DUE TIME. **KJV**

Not A Human Sacrifice?

Jehovah did not offer Jesus as a physical human sacrifice.

On the contrary, God offered Jesus to the principalities of this age as a ransom, to release the souls of mankind.

God arranged for Jesus' sinless soul to replace the sin-filled souls of mortal mankind.

Once Christ Jesus, Jesus' sinless soul, is established in a man, Christ Jesus sustains that man's physical body while he swallows up his fallen soul, the source of all disease and death.

After that, the glorified Jesus Christ is permanently joined to Christ Jesus, his Son, within that man's spiritual universe, and their unity is the source of eternal life to the flesh man.

Jesus is called a **ransom** because his spiritual life is the price that is paid in exchange for the return of Adam, God's kidnapped son.

The terms of the exchange are that the thief who stole Adam, the Son of God, the source of mankind's immortality, will be joined to Jesus, the only true source of eternal life, forever, and that God, the Father, will receive Adam, his Son, back, when he joins himself to Jesus, the last Adam, who will dwell in the earth of mankind forever, through his Son, Christ Jesus.

Jesus' spirit is outside of the people of God, and his soul, in the form of his son, Christ Jesus, is inside of the people of God. Jesus is female in relation to his father, and male in relation to his Son and to the people of God. Christ Jesus, Jesus' Son, is female in relation to the Lord Jesus, his father, and male in relation to the people of God.

The Savior of our soul is female to the glorified Elijah, who stands in front of the Spirit that is the Father of us all.

Acts 17:28 – *Children of God*

28 FOR IN HIM WE LIVE, AND MOVE, AND HAVE OUR BEING; AS CERTAIN ALSO OF YOUR OWN POETS HAVE SAID, FOR **WE ARE ALSO HIS OFFSPRING.** **KJV**

II. TO BE . . . .

Born Again?

John 3:5 – *Water And Spirit*

> 5 JESUS ANSWERED, VERILY, VERILY, I SAY UNTO THEE, EXCEPT A MAN BE **BORN OF WATER AND OF THE SPIRIT,** HE CANNOT ENTER INTO THE KINGDOM OF GOD. **KJV**

Born of Water?

Physical babies gestate is a sac filled with amniotic fluid, and are birthed into this world through that watery sac.

Born of The Spirit?

Col 1:27 – *The Female Seed*

> 27 TO WHOM GOD WOULD MAKE KNOWN WHAT IS THE RICHES OF THE GLORY OF THIS MYSTERY AMONG THE GENTILES; WHICH IS **CHRIST IN YOU,** THE HOPE OF GLORY: **KJV**

The Holy Spirit carries Christ, the female seed, which has the potential to birth Christ Jesus, the male offspring of the Lord Jesus Christ.

The Holy Spirit is transferred when one person who already has the Holy Spirit, lays their hands on another person

1 Cor 1:21 – *The Male Seed*

> 21 FOR AFTER THAT IN THE WISDOM OF GOD THE WORLD BY WISDOM KNEW NOT GOD, IT PLEASED GOD **BY THE FOOLISHNESS OF PREACHING** TO SAVE THEM THAT BELIEVE. **KJV**

After that, the male seed of the Lord Jesus Christ is transferred through the preaching of the Doctrine of Christ

Rev 12:5 – *A Male Child*

> 5 **AND SHE BROUGHT FORTH A MAN CHILD,** WHO WAS TO RULE ALL NATIONS WITH A ROD OF IRON: AND HER CHILD WAS CAUGHT UP UNTO GOD, AND TO HIS THRONE. KJV

A man is born again when he produces Christ Jesus, the spiritual male child that is the legitimate heir of the Lord Jesus Christ.

The birth of the man child is called *the new birth*, or *being reborn*, or *being born again*.

Peter 1:23 – *Incorruptible Seed*

> 23 **BEING BORN AGAIN,** NOT OF CORRUPTIBLE **SEED,** BUT OF **INCORRUPTIBLE,** BY THE WORD OF GOD, WHICH LIVETH AND ABIDETH FOR EVER. **KJV**

The incorruptible seed of the Lord Jesus Christ produces an immortal Son, Christ Jesus, who shares his immortality with the human host that he dwells in.

John 19:34 – *Blood and Water*

> 34 BUT ONE OF THE SOLDIERS WITH A SPEAR PIERCED HIS SIDE, AND **FORTHWITH CAME THERE OUT BLOOD AND WATER. KJV**

We begin to be born of the Spirit of God when the Spirit of Adoption attaches us to God through Christ, the female seed, and we are fully born again through Jesus' Blood, when the male seed of Christ Jesus is revealed through us.

2 Thess 2:8 – *The Appearance of Christ Jesus*

> 8AND THEN SHALL THAT WICKED BE REVEALED, WHOM THE LORD SHALL CONSUME WITH THE SPIRIT OF HIS MOUTH, AND SHALL DESTROY WITH **THE BRIGHTNESS OF HIS COMING: KJV**

So, the born again experience begins with the manifestation of the Spirit through the gifts of the Spirit, and ends with the manifestation, or revelation, of Christ Jesus, the male child of the Lord Jesus Christ.

Speak In Tongues?

1 Cor 12:7-10 – *Gifts Of The Spirit*

> 7 BUT THE MANIFESTATION OF **THE SPIRIT IS GIVEN TO EVERY MAN TO PROFIT WITHAL.**

> 8 FOR TO ONE IS GIVEN BY THE SPIRIT THE WORD OF WISDOM; TO ANOTHER THE WORD OF KNOWLEDGE BY THE SAME SPIRIT;

> 9 TO ANOTHER FAITH BY THE SAME SPIRIT; TO ANOTHER THE GIFTS OF HEALING BY THE SAME SPIRIT;

> 10 TO ANOTHER THE WORKING OF MIRACLES; TO ANOTHER PROPHECY; TO ANOTHER DISCERNING OF SPIRITS; TO ANOTHER DIVERS KINDS OF TONGUES; TO ANOTHER THE INTERPRETATION OF TONGUES: **KJV**

Speaking in tongues is one of the gifts that is associated with the manifestation of the Holy Spirit.

Tongues are the evidence of the *manifestation* of the Spirit, which is the beginning of *the born again experience*.

Adopted By God?

Rom 8:15-16 – *The SpiritOf Adoption*

> 15 FOR YE HAVE NOT RECEIVED THE SPIRIT OF BONDAGE AGAIN TO FEAR; BUT **YE HAVE RECEIVED THE SPIRIT OF ADOPTION, WHEREBY WE CRY, ABBA, FATHER.**
>
> 16 THE SPIRIT ITSELF BEARETH WITNESS WITH OUR SPIRIT, THAT **WE ARE THE CHILDREN OF GOD**: **KJV**

We are the adopted children of God when *The Spirit of Adoption is* attached to us, and we know that we are attached to him when our own human spirit cries out for him.

Joint Heirs With Christ?

Rom 8:17 – *Children, Heirs Of God*

> 17 AND IF CHILDREN, THEN HEIRS; HEIRS OF GOD . . .

God's adopted children are God's heirs . . .

> . . . **JOINT-HEIRS WITH CHRIST**; IF SO BE THAT WE SUFFER WITH HIM . . .

. . . as well as Christ.

We inherit everything that Christ inherits, if we suffer through the process called *tribulation*, by which Christ Jesus forces our sin nature under his authority.

> . . . THAT WE MAY BE ALSO GLORIFIED TOGETHER. **KJV**

Christ, the female seed of the Lord Jesus Christ, and mankind, are co-dependent in the beginning stage of Christ's development. Each is dependent upon the other, for continued existence.

The Christ seed dies if the man that he is attached to dies, and the man dies spiritually if the Christ seed dies.

But, if both Christ and the man live, and the Christ seed matures into the man, Christ Jesus, they will be glorified together when the Lord Jesus Christ marries Christ Jesus, his Son.

III. SALVATION . . .

Belongs To The Lord?

We cannot save our own soul. We can only submit to the Lord or resist Him, and resistance is rebellion.

<u>1 Sam 15:23</u> – *Rebellion Is Witchcraft*

> 23 FOR **REBELLION IS AS THE SIN OF WITCHCRAFT**, AND STUBBORNNESS IS AS INIQUITY AND IDOLATRY. BECAUSE THOU HAST REJECTED THE WORD OF THE LORD, HE HATH ALSO REJECTED THEE FROM BEING KING.   **KJV**

What is Jehovah=s arm? It is the soul of Messiah, the part of God that incarnated in Jesus, the man called *The Christ.*

<u>Isa 59:16</u> – *Arm Of Salvation*

> 16 AND HE SAW THAT THERE WAS NO MAN AND WONDERED THAT THERE WAS NO INTERCESSOR; THEREFORE **HIS OWN ARM BROUGHT SALVATION** UNTO HIM.   **KJV**

There are intercessors today, because Jesus Christ, the Righteous, dwells within a people who reveal his mercy.

<u>2 Cor 5:18</u> – *Ministry Of Reconciliation*

> 18 AND ALL THINGS ARE OF GOD, WHO HATH RECONCILED US TO HIMSELF BY JESUS CHRIST, AND HATH

GIVEN TO US **THE MINISTRY OF RECONCILIATION**; **KJV**

Jehovah could not find one righteous man to intercede for fallen mankind, no not one.

Rom 3:10 – *None Righteous*

10 AS IT IS WRITTEN, THERE IS **NONE RIGHTEOUS**, NO, NOT ONE: **KJV**

Aaron=s son, the High Priest, interceded for Israel on the Day of Atonement, but if he did not purify himself with the blood of goats beforehand, he and all of Israel would die.

The Spirit of God is our Lord, and God in the flesh of mankind is our King.

Zech 9:9 – *Jesus, King Of Righteousness*

9 REJOICE GREATLY, O DAUGHTER OF ZION. BEHOLD THY KING COMETH UNTO THEE. HE IS JUST AND HATH SALVATION. **KJV**

But, to be a *king*, one must have a Kingdom, and a *Kingdom* has citizens and land. So God sent His Son to appear in the flesh of Jesus of Nazareth, and the Son of God, thus, became a King. There was no one who could bring *salvation* to himself or to the rest of the mankind, so God incarnated His Son in the flesh of Jesus of Nazareth.

God did what man could not do.
He appointed a righteous king, and
gave him the authority to forgive sins.

Redeems Our Spirit?

Redemption, means, *to be purchased.*

Rom 3:24 - *Redemption in Christ Jesus*

> 24 BEING JUSTIFIED FREELY BY HIS GRACE THROUGH
> **THE REDEMPTION THAT IS IN CHRIST JESUS: KJV**

What most people understand to be **Salvation,** is called **The Common Salvation** (Jude 3). We are fully saved, spirit, soul and body, in eight steps:

The **promise of Salvation** (Eph 1:13) is for the whole man*;* **Sanctification** (2 Thess 2:13, 1 Pet 1:2) is for the human spirit, which is Jehovah's breath in mankind; **Preservation** (Lk 17:33, 2 Tim 4:18) and **Perfection** (*completion) (*Lk 8:14, 2 Cor 13:9, Heb 6:1, 7:11) are for the soul that we are born with (the personality); **Glorification** (Rom 8:17, 30) is the **moral perfection** of the spirit and the soul, and **Redemption** (Rom 8:23) and **adoption** (Rom 8:15, 23; 9:4, Gal 4:5, Eph 1:5)) are of the material body.

The final stage of the whole process of **Salvation,** is the birth of the Son of Man in an immortal body.

Jesus Christ is the **Redeemer** of our spirit, and the **Savior** of our soul. Every word in the Bible has its own meaning. They are not interchangeable.

Adam fell under the influence of the Serpent, separated from God, and died, so God sold mankind to the Serpent, the unconscious part of the carnal mind.

Rom 7:14 – *Sold Under Sin*

> 14 FOR WE KNOW THAT THE LAW IS SPIRITUAL: BUT I
> AM CARNAL, **SOLD UNDER SIN. KJV**

Rom 7:9 – *Previously Alive*

> 9 FOR **I WAS ALIVE WITHOUT THE LAW ONCE:** BUT WHEN
> THE COMMANDMENT CAME, SIN REVIVED, AND I DIED. **KJV**

The Serpent acquired Adam's human spirit, the part of mankind that was with God before the earth was founded, and now God is purchasing it by giving Christ Jesus to mankind to be our restored righteousness.

We, being the spiritual seeds of Adam's life, were righteous when we were with Adam in Eden, but we fell down with him and became encased in earthen souls engraved with the Serpent's nature, which became bodies and souls in this lower world.

God sent the Lord Jesus Christ, fallen Adam's relative, to redeem Adam's fragmented spirit, and to save the parts of Adam's soul that came into existence when Adam descended into this present world.

John 1:5 – *Light Unencumbered*

> 5 THE LIGHT SHINES IN THE DARKNESS, AND THE DARKNESS HAS NOT SUPPRESSED IT. **CJB**

Jesus is joining himself to the spirit and the soul of fallen mankind. He is adding himself to our unrighteousness, but he is not polluted by it.

1 John 5:19 – *Wicked World*

> 19 AND WE KNOW THAT WE ARE OF GOD, AND THE WHOLE WORLD LIETH IN WICKEDNESS. **KJV**

It is impossible to make Adam's fallen soul righteous, but God did the impossible.

God made Jesus, a man born of a woman, righteous, and now Jesus is doing the same thing for us. We are spiritual beings wrapped up in an unrighteous soul and body, but Jesus has forgiven us, and is purging our sins. God is doing something that is unheard of in our natural world. God is changing the heart of the sinner, rather than destroying him. He is doing it simply because he has the power to do whatever pleases Him, and it pleases Him to do so. There is no need to punish people when the power is present to purify their hearts. That is the miracle of miracles.

According to the Scripture, the natural man is sin, the exact opposite of God. God is righteous, we are unrighteous. But instead of destroying us, God is making our unrighteousness, righteous.

Rom 6:20, 33-23 - *Servants Of Sin*

20 FOR WHEN **YE WERE THE SERVANTS OF SIN**, YE WERE FREE FROM RIGHTEOUSNESS.

22 BUT **NOW BEING MADE FREE FROM SIN**, AND BECOME SERVANTS TO GOD, YE HAVE YOUR FRUIT UNTO HOLINESS, AND THE END EVERLASTING LIFE.

23 FOR **THE WAGES OF SIN IS DEATH**; BUT THE GIFT OF GOD IS ETERNAL LIFE THROUGH JESUS CHRIST OUR LORD. **KJV**

It is unfathomable and cannot be understood by the human mind. We, who are sin, shall appear in this visible world and in the world to come, as the righteous representatives of God. What an incredible miracle!

2 Cor 5:20 – *Ambassadors For Christ*

20 NOW THEN **WE ARE AMBASSADORS FOR CHRIST**, AS THOUGH GOD DID BESEECH YOU BY US: WE PRAY YOU IN CHRIST'S STEAD, BE YE RECONCILED TO GOD.   **KJV**

Do you realize what God is saying? He is telling us that we have inherited a spiritual disease that is killing us, but His seed can devour the disease and the germ that propagates it. God is making a way for us to keep our soul and become righteous without dying. Is that not incredible?

Preserves Our Soul?

Preservation is of the personality. The personality can be good, evil, or in between. The personality is *good when it is forgiven* . . .

Luke 5:24 - *Sins Forgiven*

24 BUT THAT YE MAY KNOW THAT **THE SON OF MAN HATH POWER UPON EARTH TO FORGIVE SINS,** (HE SAID UNTO THE SICK OF THE PALSY,) I SAY UNTO THEE, ARISE, AND TAKE UP THY COUCH, AND GO INTO THINE HOUSE. **KJV**

. . . evil, or a sinner, when it is separated from God,

Rom 3:23 - *Separated From God*

23 FOR **ALL HAVE SINNED**, AND COME SHORT OF THE GLORY OF GOD; **KJV**

. . .and in between, when it is seeking God for the power to become good . . .

2 Peter 3:9 - *The Lord, Long Suffering*

9 **THE LORD IS** NOT SLACK CONCERNING HIS PROMISE, AS SOME MEN COUNT SLACKNESS; BUT IS **LONGSUFFERING** TO US-WARD, NOT WILLING THAT ANY SHOULD PERISH, BUT THAT ALL SHOULD COME TO REPENTANCE. **KJV**

Jesus forgives the sins of the personality by joining his righteous male seed to it.

Matt 13:23 – *Good Ground*

23 BUT HE THAT RECEIVED SEED INTO THE GOOD GROUND IS HE THAT HEARETH THE WORD, AND UNDERSTANDETH IT; WHICH ALSO BEARETH FRUIT, AND BRINGETH FORTH, SOME AN HUNDREDFOLD, SOME SIXTY,

SOME THIRTY. **KJV**

The personality that is joined to Jesus is ***Preserved*** in the ***good***, or ***forgiven*** state, and will become ***evil***, or ***in between***, and separate from God again, only if it willfully sins.

The ***Preserved*** personality is a spiritual city that is defensed against the wicked thoughts of Satan, the unconscious part of the carnal mind, and the seducer of mankind. Satan continues to project ungodly thoughts towards the ***preserved personality***, and the ***preserved*** personality still hears those thoughts, but Satan's evil whispers bounce off the walls of the spiritual cities that Jesus defends. The Bible likens the personality and the human soul to a medieval city. In King Arthur's day, for example, cities were surrounded by walls and moats.

Curses operating in our lives are spiritual wounds that can influence the most devout believer to yield to temptation, even after they have received the power to resist. The ***preserved*** personality can still slip and fall under sin, but Satan cannot destroy it.

Num 23:23 - *No Curses Against Israel*

23 SURELY **THERE IS NO ENCHANTMENT AGAINST JACOB, NEITHER IS THERE ANY DIVINATION**_

AGAINST ISRAEL: ACCORDING TO THIS TIME IT SHALL BE SAID OF JACOB AND OF ISRAEL, WHAT HATH GOD WROUGHT! **KJV**

Israel cannot be cursed when he is ***preserved***, but he can be seduced.

Gen 3:6 – *Forbidden Fruit*

> 6 AND WHEN THE WOMAN SAW THAT THE TREE WAS
> GOOD FOR FOOD, AND THAT IT WAS PLEASANT TO THE EYES,
> AND A TREE TO BE DESIRED TO MAKE ONE WISE, SHE TOOK OF
> THE FRUIT THEREOF, **AND DID EAT, AND GAVE ALSO UNTO
> HER HUSBAND WITH HER**; AND HE DID EAT. **KJV**

We forfeit God's protection when we agree with the seducer to taste the forbidden fruit.

We have the power to reject Satan's voice once we are preserved, if we desire righteousness more than we desire the fruit.

Perfects Our Soul?

Perfection is the absence of sin.

The birth of Christ Jesus, Jesus' Son, and his union with the Lord Jesus Christ, *perfects* the human soul of the personality.

1 John 4:12 – *Love Perfected*

> 12 NO MAN HATH SEEN GOD AT ANY TIME. IF WE LOVE
> ONE ANOTHER, GOD DWELLETH IN US, AND **HIS LOVE IS
> PERFECTED IN US**. **KJV**

The *Perfected* personality, where Christ Jesus is married to the Lord Jesus, no longer hears Satan's wicked whispers.

Rev 12:5 - A *Manchid*

> 5 AND SHE BROUGHT FORTH **A MAN CHILD**, WHO WAS TO
> RULE ALL NATIONS WITH A ROD OF IRON: AND HER CHILD WAS
> CAUGHT UP UNTO GOD, AND TO HIS THRONE. **KJV**

The personality that is protected by Christ Jesus, but not yet married to the Lord Jesus, is on their way to **perfection**.

The birth of Christ Jesus rips the personalized soul out of Satan's hands and gives it the power to say, *No, Satan, I resist your thoughts*.

Adopts Our Personality?

Adoption is of the soul and its personality, which is an aspect of the human soul.

Rom 8:15 – *Spirit of Adoption*

> 15 FOR YE HAVE NOT RECEIVED THE SPIRIT OF BONDAGE AGAIN TO FEAR; BUT YE HAVE RECEIVED **THE SPIRIT OF ADOPTION**, WHEREBY WE CRY, ABBA, FATHER. **KJV**

Adoption is the translation of the lower soul into a spiritual body that can travel between the visible and spiritual worlds. The prophet Ezekiel tells us that the Zadok Priesthood wear a different garment when they minister to God, and to Israel.

We will enjoy the privilege of going before the throne of God, at will, but our soul and personality must be *adopted* first.

Sanctifies Our Spirit?

Sanctification is the separation of the human spirit from Satan, the spiritual impurity of the soul.

2 Cor 6:17 – *Unclean Thing*

> 17 WHEREFORE COME OUT FROM AMONG THEM, AND BE YE SEPARATE, SAITH THE LORD, AND TOUCH NOT **THE UNCLEAN THING**; AND I WILL RECEIVE YOU. **KJV**

Heb 4:12 – *Separation From Satan*

> 12 FOR THE WORD OF GOD IS QUICK, AND POWERFUL, AND SHARPER THAN ANY TWOEDGED SWORD, PIERCING EVEN TO THE **DIVIDING ASUNDER OF SOUL AND SPIRIT, AND OF THE JOINTS AND MARROW**, AND IS A DISCERNER OF THE THOUGHTS AND

INTENTS OF THE HEART. **KJV**

The Spirit of God attached to the fallen soul, of which we are all members, empowers the personalized soul to choose the righteous thoughts of Christ over the unrighteous thoughts of the carnal mind.

2 Tim 2:15 – *Word of Truth*

> 15 STUDY TO SHEW THYSELF APPROVED UNTO GOD, A WORKMAN THAT NEEDETH NOT TO BE ASHAMED, **RIGHTLY DIVIDING THE WORD OF TRUTH.** **KJV**

We know what is righteous, and we know what is unrighteous, because the Word of God teaches us how to distinguish between the two.

Glorifies Our Body?

Glorification is the final stage of the process called *Salvation. Glorification* is the spiritualization of the physical body and its blending with the spirit and soul into one spiritual man. *Glorification* is the seventh and final step of *Salvation*. Jesus was resurrected as one whole, spiritual man, which condition is expressed by the word, *glorified*.

Mankind must acquire an appropriate covering before we can enter into the Most Holy Place where God is.

Matt 22:12 – *No Wedding Garment*

> 12 AND HE SAITH UNTO HIM, FRIEND, HOW CAMEST THOU IN HITHER **NOT HAVING A WEDDING GARMENT**? AND HE WAS SPEECHLESS. **KJV**

Earthly bodies are not permitted before the throne of God. Jesus appeared in different forms after He was resurrected and we, too, will have the ability to take different forms after our body is glorified.

We will go up and down Jacob's ladder, back and forth between this world and the Spirit world, with impunity.

Gen 28:12 – *A Ladder On The Earth*

> 12 AND HE DREAMED, AND BEHOLD **A LADDER SET UP ON THE EARTH,** AND THE TOP OF IT REACHED TO HEAVEN: AND BEHOLD THE ANGELS OF GOD ASCENDING AND DESCENDING ON IT. **KJV**

The angels who guard the pathways will not challenge the legality of our spiritual activities, or impose any judgments associated with our going in and out of the worlds that they guard.

Makes Us Whole?

Salvation is the Greek word, ***Soteria***. It means ***rescue*** or ***safety*** from both the physical and moral effects of sin. ***Salvation*** means, ***deliverance and health***. It is from the Greek root, ***soza***, which means, ***to save, protect, heal, preserve, make whole***. Jesus' life in us, literally added to us, is the only way that we can be made whole.

Col 1:27 - *Christ in You*

> 27 TO WHOM GOD WOULD MAKE KNOWN WHAT IS THE RICHES OF THE GLORY OF THIS MYSTERY AMONG THE GENTILES; WHICH IS **CHRIST IN YOU, THE HOPE OF GLORY**: **KJV**

Salvation does not heal the fallen condition of the natural man. There is no good thing in the natural man that can be healed. Our only hope, is that life will be added to us.

Rom 8:2 – *Spirit of Life*

> 2 FOR THE LAW OF **THE SPIRIT OF LIFE IN CHRIST JESUS** HATH MADE ME FREE FROM THE LAW OF SIN AND DEATH. **KJV**

Mankind lost the Spirit of life when Adam fell and became the negative part of a mortal creation.

1 Cor 15:22 – *Death in Adam*

> 22 FOR AS **IN ADAM ALL DIE**, EVEN SO IN CHRIST SHALL ALL BE MADE ALIVE.   **KJV**

Each of us is a spiritual cosmos that can be likened to an atom. Every atom has positive and negative charges. Likewise, mankind is meant to have a positive and a negative charge. We are the negative charge, and only Christ Jesus, our positive charge, can make us a balanced atom in the body of the Lord Jesus Christ.

IV. SALVATION IS FOR . . .

The Jews?

John 4:22 – *Jewish Messiah*

> 22 YE WORSHIP YE KNOW NOT WHAT: WE KNOW
> WHAT WE WORSHIP: FOR **SALVATION IS OF THE JEWS**.   **KJV**

The Savior, Messiah, is a physical man, born of Jewish parents, whose father is a descendant of David and Solomon, of the tribe of Judah.

Rev 22:16 – *Descendant of David*

> 16 I JESUS HAVE SENT MINE ANGEL TO TESTIFY UNTO
> YOU THESE THINGS IN THE CHURCHES. **I AM THE ROOT AND
> THE OFFSPRING OF DAVID,** AND THE BRIGHT AND MORNING
> STAR.   **KJV**

The Logos, the Word of God, incarnated in the body of a natural man, Jesus of Nazareth.

Salvation is of the Jews, means that Christ, the Savior, the sinless Son of God, was birthed within Jesus of Nazareth, a Jew from the line of David.

Salvation is God in the flesh, and His flesh came from the Jews.

Jehovah called out a small group of people and gave them His law. They served Him for centuries, so by the time Jesus of

Nazareth was born, there was a minimum of curses and evil spirits on that natural flesh line that God took as his own.

Every member of the living soul that died is fallen, so it is quite a miracle that the Son of God was birthed in a human body. Christ Jesus, the Son of God, grew up with the soul man, Jesus, in Jesus> human body, and by the power of the resurrected Christ within himself, Jesus of Nazareth, purified his fallen soul.

National Israel?

Rom 1:16 – *Power To Save*

> 16 FOR I AM NOT ASHAMED OF THE GOSPEL OF CHRIST: FOR IT IS **THE POWER OF GOD UNTO SALVATION** TO EVERY ONE THAT BELIEVETH; **TO THE JEW FIRST**, AND ALSO TO THE GREEK. **KJV**

All of Abraham's descendants shall have the opportunity to appropriate the Salvation that God is offering to humanity through Jesus Christ, but all will not experience that salvation.

Rom 2:29 – *Spiritual Jew*

> 29 BUT *HE IS* A **JEW, WHICH IS ONE INWARDLY**; AND CIRCUMCISION IS THAT OF THE HEART, IN THE SPIRIT, AND NOT IN THE LETTER; WHOSE PRAISE IS NOT OF MEN, BUT OF GOD. **KJV**

The promise of *salvation* was first made to national Israel, but everyone who is born of an Israelite mother, is not an Israelite.

Acts 13:26 - *Stock of Abraham*

> 26 MEN AND BRETHREN, CHILDREN OF **THE STOCK OF ABRAHAM,** AND WHOSOEVER AMONG YOU FEARETH GOD, *TO YOU IS THE WORD OF THIS SALVATION SENT.* **KJV**

The word stock, means, *kin*, and it is from a root that means, to cause to come into being. The stock of Abraham is Christ:

Gal 3:16 – *Abraham's Nature*

> 16 NOW TO ABRAHAM AND HIS SEED, WERE THE PROMISES MADE, NOT SEEDS AS OF MANY, BUT ONE, AND TO **THY SEED WHICH IS CHRIST.**   KJV

The promise of Salvation is spiritual and the fulfillment of the promise is spiritual. All of national Israel will have the opportunity to be saved from death, but it is up to the individual to believe that eternal life is possible, to desire it, and to pursue God until he acquires it.

Spiritual Israel?

Gal 6:16 – *Israel of God*

> 16 AND AS MANY AS WALK ACCORDING TO THIS RULE, PEACE BE ON THEM, AND MERCY, AND UPON **THE ISRAEL OF GOD.**   KJV

The citizens of Spiritual Israel are defined by their spiritual ancestors, not by their human bloodlines. Everyone who has the spiritual blood of Jesus Christ is a spiritual Israelite. The Blood of Jesus is in Christ, Jesus' female seed, the believer's potential to birth the manchild.

The grafting of Christ to our fallen nature can be likened to the Israelites placing the blood of the paschal lamb on their doorposts. That blood identified them as ***protected persons to*** the Angel of Death that Jehovah sent to destroy the first born of Egypt.

The glorified Jesus Christ is reproducing Himself in spiritual Israel. Each spiritual Israelite is a womb where the male mind of Christ Jesus, His Son, can be formed.

Rev 12:5 – *Male Mind*

> 5 AND **SHE BROUGHT FORTH A MAN CHILD**, WHO WAS TO RULE ALL NATIONS WITH A ROD OF IRON: AND HER CHILD WAS CAUGHT UP UNTO GOD, AND TO HIS THRONE.
> **KJV**

God always chooses the spiritual over the natural brother. It is a Scriptural principle that when there are two, God chooses the spiritual over the natural. There is a natural and a spiritual seed of Israel, and the spiritual seed is *Christ*.

The Law of Moses justifies the natural Jew, but it cannot save his soul, because sacrificing bulls and goats *does not purify the conscience*.

Messiah is the only way to go beyond the righteousness that is attainable through the Law.

In other words, a relationship with *the Lord Jesus Christ* is the only way to lay hold of the *promises of God*. Jew and Gentile, alike, must come to God as spiritual Israel, through the seed of Christ, which has made *salvation* available to the entire world.

The Jewish people do not recognize that Jesus Christ is Messiah, but God Almighty is great enough to deliver His People. He will remove the veil from their eyes in His own time.

Rom 11:25 - *Blinded by Satan - 1*

> 25 FOR I WOULD NOT BRETHREN, THAT YE SHOULD BE IGNORANT OF THIS MYSTERY, LEST YOU SHOULD BE WISE IN YOUR OWN CONCEIT; THAT **BLINDNESS**, IN PART, **HAS HAPPENED TO ISRAEL**, UNTIL THE FULLNESS OF THE GENTILES BE COME IN. AND SO **ALL ISRAEL SHALL BE SAVED.**
> **KJV**

Salvation is a mystery, and the mystery is that the seed of Jesus Christ, Messiah, in us, is our personal hope of eternal life. . .
.

Col 1:27 – *The Internalized Christ - 1*

> 27 TO WHOM GOD WOULD MAKE KNOWN WHAT IS
> THE RICHES OF THE GLORY OF THIS MYSTERY AMONG THE
> GENTILES; WHICH IS **CHRIST IN YOU, THE HOPE OF GLORY**:
> **KJV**

Our natural heritage cannot save us. Jewish parents cannot save us. Christian parents cannot save us. We stand or fall by the spiritual life that dwells within us.

Rom 8:9-10 - *The Internalized Christ - 2*

> 9 BUT YE ARE NOT IN THE FLESH, BUT IN THE SPIRIT, IF
> SO BE THAT THE SPIRIT OF GOD DWELL IN YOU. NOW IF ANY
> MAN HAVE NOT THE SPIRIT OF CHRIST, HE IS NONE OF HIS.
>
> 10 AND **IF CHRIST BE IN YOU**, THE BODY IS DEAD
> BECAUSE OF SIN; BUT **THE SPIRIT IS LIFE** BECAUSE OF
> RIGHTEOUSNESS. **KJV**

All of natural Israel is not spiritual Israel, but some day they will, indeed, be grafted back into their own Tree.

Rom 11:24 – *Israel Grafted In*

> 24 FOR IF THOU WERT CUT OUT OF THE OLIVE TREE
> WHICH IS WILD BY NATURE, AND WERT GRAFFED CONTRARY
> TO NATURE INTO A GOOD OLIVE TREE: HOW MUCH MORE
> SHALL THESE, WHICH BE THE NATURAL BRANCHES, BE
> **GRAFFED INTO THEIR OWN OLIVE TREE**? **KJV**

The Word of God, *Salvation*, is available to the Jews. They are not locked out, but *Salvation* is only in the Name of Jesus Christ, our Messiah. The veil must be lifted off of their eyes, if they are to experience the salvation of God.

2 Cor 3:13-16 - *Blinded By Satan - 2*

> 13 AND NOT AS **MOSES, WHICH PUT A VAIL OVER
> HIS FACE**, THAT THE CHILDREN OF ISRAEL COULD NOT
> STEADFASTLY LOOK TO THE END OF THAT WHICH IS

ABOLISHED:

> 14 BUT THEIR MINDS WERE BLINDED: **FOR UNTIL THIS DAY REMAINETH THE SAME VAIL UNTAKEN AWAY IN THE READING OF THE OLD TESTAMENT**; WHICH VAIL IS DONE AWAY IN CHRIST.

> 15 BUT EVEN UNTO THIS DAY, WHEN MOSES IS READ, **THE VAIL IS UPON THEIR HEART.**

> 16 NEVERTHELESS **WHEN IT SHALL TURN TO THE LORD, THE VAIL SHALL BE TAKEN AWAY. KJV**

If you are a natural Jew hearing this Word, and you desire the truth but cannot understand the message of God's Salvation through Jesus Christ, ask God for the understanding. He will not withhold any good thing from you.

God did not blind the Jews so that the Gentiles could be saved. Satan, the god of this world, blinded them.

<u>2 Cor 4:4</u> – *Blinded by Satan - 3*

> 4 IN WHOM **THE GOD OF THIS WORLD HATH BLINDED THE MINDS OF THEM WHICH BELIEVE NOT**, LEST THE LIGHT OF THE GLORIOUS GOSPEL OF CHRIST, WHO IS THE IMAGE OF GOD, SHOULD SHINE UNTO THEM. **KJV**

The Gentiles?

<u>Rom 11:11</u> – *Gentiles Saved - 1*

> 11 BUT RATHER THROUGH THE FALL OF THE JEWS, **SALVATION IS COME UNTO THE GENTILES. KJV**

<u>Acts 28:28</u> - *Gentiles Saved - 2*

> 28 **THE SALVATION OF GOD IS SENT UNTO THE GENTILES. KJV**

The definition of **Gentiles** is, *a company, a troop, a multitude*, but it really means the people outside of the consecrated nation of Israel. God created a living soul, and it died, but the female element of the creation continues to exist in a hostile, war-like state against God.

The soul that died is filled with sin and paganism, so God came down to this world and chose a little nation called Israel to justify and consecrate by giving them His Law. But, Israel hardened their heart and sinned against God, so He took the Word of His *Gospel of Salvation*, and gave it to the raging, heathen masses.

Acts 11:18 – *Gentiles Granted Repentance*

> 18 WHEN THEY HEARD THESE THINGS, THEY HELD THEIR PEACE, AND GLORIFIED GOD, SAYING, THEN HATH **GOD ALSO TO THE GENTILES GRANTED REPENTANCE UNTO LIFE.** **KJV**

After the Gentiles experience *Salvation*, this Word of the Gospel is going back to the Jews, and, at that time, all Israel shall be saved

Rom 11:26 – *All Israel Saved*

> 26 AND SO **ALL ISRAEL SHALL BE SAVED**: AS IT IS WRITTEN, THERE SHALL COME OUT OF SION THE DELIVERER, AND SHALL TURN AWAY UNGODLINESS FROM JACOB: **KJV**

This Scripture is talking about *spiritual Israel*, those who are called in natural Israel, and those who are called of the Gentiles.

Israel are the bodies that the spiritual seed of God dwells in, so everyone who has been incarnated at the express will of the Father is spiritual Israel. Those who have been incarnated illegally, at the express will of the fallen soul, are not spiritual Israel. Those who have been incarnated illegally, can still live out their lives, and have a positive experience. It could be a very good life. But when that body and soul die, they will not enter into life because they were born before their appointed time to experience the world to come. The bodies go back to the dust, and the soul must wait until God calls it to eternal life.

Every soul is invited to be saved, but the body the soul lives in must come in the order that God calls it. It is illegal to come into this world without permission. If we get here illegally, we can have a decent life, but we will not receive the fruit of creation, which is eternal life.

All Flesh?

Luke 3:5-6 - *All Flesh Saved*

> 5 EVERY VALLEY SHALL BE FILLED, AND EVERY MOUNTAIN AND HILL SHALL BE BROUGHT LOW; AND THE CROOKED SHALL BE MADE STRAIGHT, AND THE ROUGH WAYS SHALL BE MADE SMOOTH;

> 6 AND **ALL FLESH SHALL SEE THE SALVATION OF GOD**. **KJV**

The root of the entire living soul will be saved, but the individual has to wait until God calls him. This is what God is talking about, when He says, *the valley shall be filled, and the mountains shall be brought low.*

We are waiting to be completed, because we are half a creation. We are spiritual valleys. We are lacking something, and Jesus is filling in what is missing. He is filling in all the valleys with his own spiritual substance, and we will be whole.

The natural man who is high in his own estimation, will be brought low. God makes no qualms about saying that the natural man is lifted up in pride, which God describes as *mountains*. The proud do not become glorified creations. These mountains would not let the Spirit of God in. The Spirit of God came to them, and they put up defenses against Him, saying, we do not want you. Pride must come down, if the Spirit of God is to enter.

God is making these mountains even. He will enter in, by His Spirit, and put everything on an even keel. The peace that God promises us is emotional peace. When we get excited, our heart rate increases. This can be picked up by an electrocardiogram. When we get excited, our heart rate increases and spikes appear on the read-out. We are not supposed to look like that when we are in Christ. When we are a complete creation, our read-out will be flat, peace.

No matter what happens over here in the realm of appearance, no matter what comes against us, we are supposed to remain even. Maybe arrows and darts are coming against us. When we are a complete creation, they just bounce off. When we are an incomplete creation, when we are half-way created, we have moments of peace because we do have Christ. But then the dart comes against us, and we get all upset. The dart gets us, and we manifest and retaliate. Someone punches us in the face, and we stop loving him.

We must have the power of Christ in our life to have peace. We know that we are a completed creation when we no longer have emotional or ungodly reactions to the darts that come against us. No more mountains.

Every emotional or ungodly reaction is the result of pride. If someone comes against us and says, *I hate you*, and we get upset, it is pride. Even if the issue is extreme, like *you stole my husband*. If we manifest emotional or ungodly behavior, it is pride. Those mountains are coming down because we know that, no matter what comes against us, there is nothing that this soul realm can steal from us, that God will not restore, two fold.

Moving into that revelation is the only true peace. We would have it made, if we could just believe that.

Now, that does not mean that we give everything that we own away. It means that we do everything that we can, in righteousness, to help others. We do not give away our last dollar. We do what is right. We try to give needy people a break, a leg up.

We try to help them, and believe that God will vindicate us. We must believe that we will not be destroyed by doing good. We must be willing to lose everything for God, knowing that He will keep us from destruction. There is no other way to go, brethren. We have to be willing to lose everything, believing that God is our defense in righteous-ness.

The Ends of The Earth?

Acts 13:47 – *Ends of The Earth*

47 I HAVE SET THEE TO BE A LIGHT OF THE GENTILES THAT THOU SHOULD BE FOR **SALVATION UNTO THE ENDS OF THE EARTH**. **KJV**

This is a very controversial Scripture. *The ends of the earth* can be likened to the controversy over outer darkness. I have heard Christians talking about *outer darkness* being a planet, or something like that.

We are a living soul. Our body is the house of our soul. Our spiritual substance is deep within our heart. We have a spirit, and we have a soul. The flesh is both the soul and the body. They are both made out of spiritual dust.

We measure a man from his innermost spiritual being, to his outermost spiritual being. *Outer darkness*, is the place that is farthest away from the spirit. It is as far away as you can go from the center, to the outermost point on the circumference of that man. It is the most exterior spiritual place that one can be. It is the place that is farthest away from the spirit.

When Christ Jesus comes, he joins himself to our spirit. That means he is inside of you. If you have Christ, he is inside of you. *Outer darkness* or *the ends of the earth* is inside of you. *Outer darkness* or *the ends of the earth* is not Mars. It is the physical body. We need a spiritual mind to understand the Scripture. *Outer darkness* is not Mars.

64

God is making a creation, and everything that He talks about concerns His creation. ***The ends of the earth*** is our physical body. Our body will be ***adopted.*** Our spiritual body, our mind, is being ***saved***, and our spirit is being ***redeemed***. The whole creation is being apprehended by the Lord Jesus Christ.

V. SALVATION IS . . .

A Prince?

Salvation is Elohim, God, the Creator, within mankind, the vessels he formed to house his Spirit.

Mankind, Adam, is alive when God occupies him, but the vessels die when they depart from their source of life.

Acts 17:28 – *God in All*

> 28 FOR **IN HIM WE LIVE, AND MOVE, AND HAVE OUR BEING;** AS CERTAIN ALSO OF YOUR OWN POETS HAVE SAID, FOR WE ARE ALSO HIS OFFSPRING.   **KJV**

Spiritual life inside of mankind is called *angel*. Some angels exist only for the lifetime of their host, and have no personal name. These lower angels are called kings. Other higher angels, called archangels, have personal names such as *Michael* and *Gabriel*.

Then, there is a spiritual office higher than *angel*. God inside of a man is called *Prince*.

Jesus is an Adam, a member of mankind. Jesus is the first mortal man to be restored to life when the Son of God possessed his vessel.

67

Rev 1:5 – *First Reborn*

> 5 AND FROM JESUS CHRIST, WHO IS THE FAITHFUL
> WITNESS, AND THE FIRST BEGOTTEN OF THE DEAD, AND THE
> PRINCE OF THE KINGS OF THE EARTH. UNTO HIM THAT LOVED
> US, AND WASHED US FROM OUR SINS IN HIS OWN BLOOD, **KJV**

Righteous Adam, the Prince inside of Jesus, joined with the man, Jesus, so completely that Jesus became the vehicle that performs the actions of God. Elohim, God, and Jesus, his vessel, are entering into mankind today, to give them life, and, as such, God and Jesus, his vessel, are called by one Name, the Name of God in a man, the Prince of Life.

Acts 3:15 – *The Prince Of Life*

> 15 AND KILLED **THE PRINCE OF LIFE,** WHOM GOD
> HATH RAISED FROM THE DEAD; WHEREOF WE ARE WITNESSES.
> **KJV**

Salvation, the Prince of Life, is the Lord Jesus Christ, and he has two aspects, soul and spirit, or vessel and inner man.

High forms of spiritual life are hermaphroditical. They are both sexes. The Lord Jesus Christ is both male and female. The Spirit of God that makes Jesus a Prince is his spirit, which is male, and his Adam, or soul side, is female.

Song 2:9 – *The Prince Behind The Saviour*

> 9 MY BELOVED IS LIKE A ROE OR A YOUNG HART:
> BEHOLD, HE STANDETH BEHIND OUR WALL, **HE LOOKETH
> FORTH AT THE WINDOWS, SHEWING HIMSELF THROUGH
> THE LATTICE. KJV**

Jehovah is the Name of God that communicates with Israel, and one of His appellations is *the Breasted One* that brings up children. God is revealing Himself through the Name *Jehovah* and through the man, Christ Jesus, today, to save mankind.

A Captain?

Heb 2:10 – *Jesus, Our Captain*

> 10 FOR IT BECAME HIM, FOR WHOM ARE ALL THINGS, AND BY WHOM ARE ALL THINGS, IN BRINGING MANY SONS UNTO GLORY, TO MAKE THE **CAPTAIN OF THEIR SALVATION** PERFECT THROUGH SUFFERINGS. **KJV**

Jesus is the author of eternal salvation, the *salvation* by which we experience the immortal life of the ages.

Heb 5:9 – *Jesus, Perfect*

> 9 AND **BEING MADE PERFECT,** HE BECAME THE AUTHOR OF ETERNAL SALVATION UNTO ALL THEM THAT OBEY HIM. **KJV**

The words, *Captain* and *Author* are two translations of the same Greek word, which means, *the commencement, or the chief, or the beginning*.

Christ is the beginning of our salvation. When Christ comes to dwell in us, it is the beginning of the process that results in the *Salvation of our soul. There is no Salvation outside of Jesus*. He is the beginning. If we do not have a relationship with Jesus, we have no reason to hope for Salvation.

A Promise?

The Promise of the Holy Spirit is the beginning of our faith. It is not true that once you have the *Promise*, you have it all. The truth is that the Holy Spirit is the beginning of a very long process that ends in our glorification, which is the translation of our physical body into a spiritual body.

1 Cor 15:38-44 – *A Spiritual Body*

> 38 BUT GOD GIVETH IT A BODY AS IT HATH PLEASED HIM, AND TO EVERY SEED HIS OWN BODY.

42 SO ALSO IS THE RESURRECTION OF THE DEAD. IT IS SOWN IN CORRUPTION; IT IS RAISED IN INCORRUPTION:

44 IT IS SOWN A NATURAL BODY; IT IS RAISED A SPIRITUAL BODY. **THERE IS A NATURAL BODY, AND THERE IS A SPIRITUAL BODY. KJV**

How is our soul being saved?

<u>Ps 3:8</u> *– Salvation Of The Lord*

8 **SALVATION BELONGETH UNTO THE LORD**: THY BLESSING IS UPON THY PEOPLE. SELAH. **KJV**

Some look within their own selves for **Salvation**. They believe that they were called from before the earth was founded and that their human spirit, alone, without being joined to the glorified Jesus Christ, can birth the Christ of their **Salvation**. They call it **the enabling**. They believe that if they could only find the part of themselves that was with God from the beginning that Christ would appear within them to save their soul.

<u>1 Cor 12:28</u> *– Five-Fold Ministry*

28 AND GOD HATH SET SOME IN THE CHURCH, FIRST **APOSTLES, SECONDARILY PROPHETS, THIRDLY TEACHERS,** AFTER THAT MIRACLES, THEN GIFTS OF HEALINGS, HELPS, GOVERNMENTS, DIVERSITIES OF TONGUES. **KJV**

A Process?

Salvation is a process that rescues the soul from the influence of Satan, the unconscious part of the carnal mind. We no longer hear the wicked whispers of the Serpent when our spirit and soul are fully **saved**, because the process that saves the soul destroys Satan and Leviathan, who are the ancient Serpent in this age.

Salvation begins with the rescue of our soul. Jesus snatches us from the clutches of Satan, the unconscious part of the carnal mind. After that, we receive power to oppose Satan=s thoughts and impulses.

<u>Acts 1:8</u> – *Power Of The Holy Ghost*

8 BUT YE SHALL RECEIVE POWER, AFTER THAT THE HOLY GHOST IS COME UPON YOU: AND YE SHALL BE WITNESSES UNTO ME BOTH IN JERUSALEM, AND IN ALL JUDAEA, AND IN SAMARIA, AND UNTO THE UTTERMOST PART OF THE EARTH. **KJV**

Salvation makes us a defensed city. The Spirit of God builds Christ in us, and Christ Jesus, the Son of God, emerges in layers that surround the soul like a spiritual wall.

<u>Eph 6:11-17</u> – *Armor Of God*

11 PUT ON **THE WHOLE ARMOUR OF GOD**, THAT YE MAY BE ABLE TO STAND AGAINST THE WILES OF THE DEVIL.

12 FOR **WE WRESTLE NOT AGAINST FLESH AND BLOOD**, BUT AGAINST PRINCIPALITIES, AGAINST POWERS, AGAINST THE RULERS OF THE DARKNESS OF THIS WORLD, AGAINST SPIRITUAL WICKEDNESS IN HIGH PLACES.

13 WHEREFORE TAKE UNTO YOU **THE WHOLE ARMOUR OF GOD**, THAT YE MAY BE ABLE TO WITHSTAND IN THE EVIL DAY, AND HAVING DONE ALL, TO STAND.

14 STAND THEREFORE, HAVING YOUR LOINS GIRT ABOUT WITH TRUTH, AND HAVING ON **THE BREASTPLATE OF RIGHTEOUSNESS;**

15 AND YOUR FEET SHOD WITH THE PREPARATION OF **THE GOSPEL OF PEACE;**

16 ABOVE ALL, TAKING **THE SHIELD OF FAITH**, WHEREWITH YE SHALL BE ABLE TO QUENCH ALL THE FIERY DARTS OF THE WICKED.

17 AND TAKE *THE HELMET OF SALVATION*, AND THE SWORD OF THE SPIRIT, WHICH IS THE WORD OF GOD: **KJV**

Some believers put on their spiritual armor every morning, but saying the words are not enough. God would surely honor us for trying, because that kind of faith is beautiful to behold, but we cannot don the armor of God with words. It has to be built into us through the faith of the Son of God. Our armor has to be born into our spiritual being.

Christ Jesus, the armor of God, when applied with faith, empowers us to overcome the temptation to sin.

Forgiveness?

Jesus subdued the unrighteousness of the living soul that died, and brought it into submission to the righteousness of the Spirit of God.

The human spirit in the fallen Adamic race is a relative of God, but she has been completely overtaken by Satan, the unconscious part of the carnal mind, and has been spiritually fornicating with him for centuries. She is incapable of lifting herself up from the depths of unrighteousness to redeem the living soul that died. The human spirit is, indeed, the Christ, but she is dead because she is married to Satan, the spirit that rules mankind through the unconscious part of the carnal mind.

Eph 2:2 – *Prince of The Power Of The Air*

2 WHEREIN IN TIME PAST YE WALKED ACCORDING TO THE COURSE OF THIS WORLD, ACCORDING TO **THE PRINCE OF THE POWER OF THE AIR, THE SPIRIT THAT NOW WORKETH IN THE CHILDREN OF DISOBEDIENCE. KJV**

So God sent His Son to regenerate the human spirit, which is the dead Christ, in the many members of fallen humanity. But, Satan, the military power of the soul, which is completely opposed to the Son of God, stands between Christ Jesus and the human spirit in a man, to prevent its resurrection from the dead.

Acts 13:8 – *Elymas, The Sorcerer*

8 BUT **ELYMAS THE SORCERER** (FOR SO IS HIS NAME BY INTERPRETATION) **WITHSTOOD THEM,** SEEKING TO TURN AWAY THE DEPUTY FROM THE FAITH. **KJV**

The last Adam in the person of Jesus of Nazareth . . .

1 Cor 15:45 – *The Last Adam*

45 AND SO IT IS WRITTEN, THE FIRST MAN ADAM WAS MADE A LIVING SOUL; **THE LAST ADAM** WAS MADE A QUICKENING SPIRIT. **KJV**

. . . brought the criminal living soul that died into submission, and by the power of Christ Jesus, put Satan, the unconscious part of the mind underfoot.

Rom 1:4 – *Spirit of Holiness*

4 AND DECLARED TO BE THE SON OF GOD WITH POWER, ACCORDING TO THE SPIRIT OF HOLINESS, BY THE RESURRECTION FROM THE DEAD: **KJV**

Jesus of Nazareth, having succeeded in dominating the living soul that died, received the power and authority to impart the spirit of Holiness to the remainder of mankind, so that we might do the same.

Luke 10:19 – *Power Over Witchcraft*

19 BEHOLD, **I GIVE UNTO YOU POWER** TO TREAD ON SERPENTS AND SCORPIONS, AND OVER ALL THE POWER OF THE ENEMY: AND NOTHING SHALL BY ANY MEANS HURT YOU. **KJV**

Jesus joined the two Adams, the fallen Adam and Christ Jesus, the last Adam, in the vessel, known as Jesus of Nazareth.

Eph 2:15 – *One Man*

> 15 HAVING ABOLISHED IN HIS FLESH THE ENMITY, EVEN THE LAW OF COMMANDMENTS CONTAINED IN ORDINANCES; **FOR TO MAKE IN HIMSELF OF TWAIN ONE NEW MAN,** SO MAKING PEACE;   **KJV**

The new man is Christ Jesus, who is ascended to his Father, and, by his ascension, the same victory is available to the rest of mankind. The hard part is over. All we have to do is appropriate Jesus' victory in our vessel.

On the other hand, it is difficult to believe that the hard part is over as we experience the trials and tribulations of overcoming our carnal mind. But the fact is that one man, Jesus of Nazareth, overcame sin, and by Christ Jesus, the strength of his victory, we inherit his faith to overcome, as well.

2 Peter 1:1 – *Precious Faith*

> 1 SIMON PETER, A SERVANT AND AN APOSTLE OF JESUS CHRIST, TO THEM THAT HAVE OBTAINED **LIKE PRECIOUS FAITH** WITH US **THROUGH THE RIGHTEOUSNESS OF GOD AND OUR SAVIOUR JESUS CHRIST:**   **KJV**

Jesus made a way for mankind to return to the Father, so why should we think about hard times, when we can look ahead to victory and glory in the Spirit of God.

Eternal Life?

Salvation is eternal life, without sorrow. We are saved from death and hell, which is this world system, through union with Jehovah, the source of life. Jesus is the only one who came near to God and lived, so common men can now draw close to Jehovah through a relationship with Jesus Christ.

<u>1 Peter 1:9</u> – *The Outcome Of Faith*

> 9 RECEIVING **THE END OF YOUR FAITH, EVEN THE SALVATION OF YOUR SOULS.** **KJV**

The *salvation* of our soul is the end of our faith. What is the beginning of our faith?

<u>Acts 2:33</u> – *Promise of The Holy Ghost*

> 33 THEREFORE BEING BY THE RIGHT HAND OF GOD EXALTED, AND HAVING RECEIVED OF THE FATHER **THE PROMISE OF THE HOLY GHOST**, HE HATH SHED FORTH THIS, WHICH YE NOW SEE AND HEAR. **KJV**

<u>John 1:1-4</u> – *In The Beginning*

> 1 IN THE BEGINNING WAS THE WORD, AND THE WORD WAS WITH GOD, AND THE WORD WAS GOD.
>
> 2 THE SAME WAS IN THE BEGINNING WITH GOD.
>
> 3 **ALL THINGS WERE MADE BY HIM**; AND WITHOUT HIM WAS NOT ANY THING MADE THAT WAS MADE.
>
> 4 **IN HIM WAS LIFE**; AND THE LIFE WAS THE LIGHT OF MEN. **KJV**

But the Truth is that we are not whole; *something has to be added to us*, which is the very definition of *Salvation*. So, we see that they desire the *Salvation* of God, but deny the power of God that is necessary to attain it.

<u>2 Tim 3:5</u> – *The Power Of God Denied*

> 5 HAVING A FORM OF GODLINESS, **BUT DENYING THE POWER THEREOF**: FROM SUCH TURN AWAY. **KJV**

1 John 2:22 – *Father & Son Denied*

> 22 WHO IS A LIAR BUT HE THAT DENIETH THAT JESUS IS THE CHRIST? **HE IS ANTICHRIST, THAT DENIETH THE FATHER AND THE SON. KJV**

God sent Jesus to tell the world this glorious Truth, that the Lord Jesus Christ is in the process of creating mankind in the image of Jehovah and that it is his work, which means that it is not necessary to use mind control to attain it. We have only to commit ourselves to study faithfully, and fearlessly confront and resist our own sin nature.

They are also saying that the Church no longer needs teachers, but that day will not come until there are no more students.

A Shield & A Horn?

2 Sam 22:3 – *Jesus, Our Shield*

> 3 THE GOD OF MY ROCK; IN HIM WILL I TRUST: HE IS **MY SHIELD, AND THE HORN OF MY SALVATION**, MY HIGH TOWER, AND MY REFUGE, MY SAVIOUR; THOU SAVEST ME FROM VIOLENCE. **KJV**

Shields are defenses against spiritual powers. In Bible days, they made vessels out of horns. They would hollow them out and keep things in them. So a horn has a hard, defensive exterior.

Our soul is becoming defensed, like a defensed city, so that the thoughts of Satan, the unconscious part of the carnal mind, cannot cause us to sin. Our physical body will become a hard, defensive exterior around our mind. It will not get sick. It will not be damaged. It will not be gangrenous, and it will not corrupt in any manner, shape, or form.

2 Sam 22:51 – *Jesus, Our Tower*

> 51 HE IS **THE TOWER OF SALVATION** FOR HIS KING:
> AND SHEWETH MERCY TO HIS ANOINTED, UNTO DAVID, AND
> TO HIS SEED FOR EVERMORE. **KJV**

Jesus is our tower, a safe place within the vulnerable areas of our emotions and physical bodies.

The powers of this world come against new believers with a vengeance, sometimes attacking their souls and their bodies, without mercy, for long periods of time. They attack our lives and our emotions. The more bound we are when we come to the Lord, the longer it takes to find the much-desired, promised peace.

But at all times, from the moment that we receive *the Promise of Salvation*, there is a place in the deepest recesses of our spiritual being that God describes as *a tower*. It is not a physical tower. It is a spiritual place that God describes as a tower. In the past, a tower with a wall around it was always built in the midst of a city, so that, in the event that an invading force tore down the wall and entered the city, everyone could run into the tower. Every city had a tower to protect the townspeople. That tower was the last bastion of defense for the people, after the wall was knocked down.

From the day we receive *the Promise of Salvation*, we have a spiritual tower that we can run into while our body, soul and spirit are still weak, and that tower is within us. We can get down on our face before God and cry out for help, and Jesus will deliver us every time.

Prov 18:14 – *Wounded Spirit*

> 14 THE SPIRIT OF A MAN WILL SUSTAIN HIS
> INFIRMITY; BUT **A WOUNDED SPIRIT WHO CAN BEAR**? **KJV**

It is not very popular to preach that the spirit can still be weak after we receive *the Promise of Salvation*, but that is the truth. Our spirit can be breached. It can be damaged. We can be damaged on all three levels, body, soul and spirit, but in the midst of it all, Jesus can enter into our spiritual universe, like a man of war, and be a tower inside of us. We can turn to Jesus with any problem. He will deliver us every time we are attacked, and we will overcome and move on to victory.

A Wall?

Isa 26:1 – *Jesus, Our Wall*

> 1 IN THAT DAY SHALL THIS SONG BE SUNG IN THE LAND OF JUDAH; WE HAVE A STRONG CITY; **SALVATION WILL GOD APPOINT FOR WALLS AND BULWARKS.** **KJV**

In the third stage of the *Salvation of our soul*, when Christ Jesus has totally joined himself to us and swallowed up Satan, the unconscious part of the carnal mind, Christ Jesus will be a wall to our spiritually powerless city. No one, spirit or man, will be able to climb over Christ Jesus. We shall be a defensed city when our *Salvation* is perfected.

Hope?

1 Thess 5:8 - *Jesus, Our Hope*

> 8 BUT LET US, WHO ARE OF THE DAY, BE SOBER, PUTTING ON THE BREAST-PLATE OF FAITH AND LOVE; AND FOR AN HELMET, **THE HOPE OF SALVATION.** **KJV**

Titus 2:13 – *Jesus, The Blessed Hope*

> 13 LOOKING FOR **THAT BLESSED HOPE,** AND THE GLORIOUS APPEARING OF THE GREAT GOD AND OUR SAVIOUR JESUS CHRIST. **KJV**

The human spirit needs to be protected because the mind is formed around the human spirit. When Christ Jesus controls the human spirit, the mind of that person is the Christ Mind. But when Satan controls the human spirit, the mind of that man is carnal, the mind of the flesh, called *the carnal mind*.

The human spirit can be breached, but Christ Jesus is a spiritual helmet that protects our human spirit, and forms it into the Christ mind.

Christ inside us is our hope of Salvation, because God is saving mankind one man at a time, by adding Christ Jesus to our personal spiritual universe. Christ Jesus is our personal Savior.

A Garment?

Isa 61:10 – *Christ Jesus, Our Clothing*

> 10 I WILL GREATLY REJOICE IN THE LORD, MY SOUL SHALL BE JOYFUL IN MY GOD; FOR **HE HATH CLOTHED ME WITH THE GARMENTS OF SALVATION,** HE HATH COVERED ME WITH THE ROBE OF RIGHTEOUSNESS, AS A BRIDEGROOM DECKETH HIMSELF WITH ORNAMENTS, AND AS A BRIDE ADORNETH HERSELF WITH HER JEWELS. **KJV**

Salvation is life in the visible world. Spirits are not saved. Spirits are redeemed. Souls are saved. Christ Jesus clothes our soul with eternal life in the visible world. *Salvation is a garment* that covers our naked sin nature, so that we can appear in the world to come without corruption.

A Well?

Isa 12:3 – *Jesus, Saviour Of The Emotions*

> 3 THEREFORE WITH JOY SHALL YE DRAW WATER OUT OF **THE WELLS OF SALVATION.** **KJV**

Each human being is a microcosm of Sheol, the pit in which God is developing His creation. *The pit* is the consciousness of the soul.

In the beginning, that pit contains the animal nature of the creation, but it becomes a *Well of Salvation* when the spiritual life of God swallows up mankind's potential to sin, and shines forth from the deep its waters.

A Cup?

Ps 116:13 – *Jesus, Saviour of The Body*

> 13 I WILL TAKE **THE CUP OF SALVATION**, AND CALL UPON THE NAME OF THE LORD. **KJV**

Our physical body is the cup that is being created to hold the spiritual life of God.

Joy?

Ps 51:12 – *Spiritual Joy*

> 12 RESTORE UNTO ME **THE JOY OF THY SALVATION;** AND UPHOLD ME WITH THY FREE SPIRIT. **KJV**

The joy of the Lord is a spiritual joy. It is not emotional. We experience spiritual joy through a relationship with Christ Jesus, the Son of God, which is based upon *the Word of God*. A relationship that is based upon spirit and spiritual experiences only, is not likely to be of God.

Great?

Heb 2:2-3 – *No Rapture*

> 2 FOR IF THE WORD SPOKEN BY ANGELS WAS STEADFAST AND **EVERY TRANSGRESSION AND DISOBEDIENCE RECEIVED A JUST RECOMPENSE** OF REWARD,

> 3 HOW SHALL WE ESCAPE, IF WE NEGLECT **SO GREAT A SALVATION,** WHICH AT THE FIRST, BEGAN TO BE SPOKEN BY THE LORD AND WAS CONFIRMED UNTO US, BY THEM THAT HEARD HIM. **KJV**

What should we do? Should we wait passively for the Lord to carry us away? No. God has given us the strength to overcome the spiritual military power of our carnal mind. Our part is to join Christ Jesus in his battle to overthrow our sin nature.

Christ Jesus, our personal Savior, is great enough to overcome any obstacle that Satan, the enemy of our soul can throw in our path.

Confession?

<u>Rom 10:10</u> – *Confession Necessary*

> 10 FOR WITH THE HEART MAN BELIEVETH UNTO RIGHTEOUSNESS; AND WITH THE MOUTH **CONFESSION IS MADE UNTO SALVATION. KJV**

We must confess our sins. We cannot live behind a wall of fantasy. We must confess the wickedness of our soul, because, as long as we deny it, there will be no healing or deliverance for us. Judgment, alone, will hang over our lives like a canopy, and pride will be our garment.

Repentance?

<u>2 Cor 7:10</u> – *Sorrow To Repentance*

> 10 FOR **GODLY SORROW WORKETH REPENTANCE TO SALVATION** NOT TO BE REPENTED OF: BUT THE SORROW OF THE WORLD WORKETH DEATH. **KJV**

Only God can convict us of sin and help us to sorrow to the point that He grants us repentance.

Repentance that is not preceded by sorrow is a false repentance.

<u>Acts 5:31</u> – *Repentance For Israel*

> 31 HIM HATH GOD EXALTED WITH HIS RIGHT HAND TO BE A PRINCE AND A SAVIOUR, FOR TO GIVE **REPENTANCE TO ISRAEL**, AND FORGIVENESS OF SINS. **KJV**

Self-Judgment?

Phil 2:12 – *Individual Responsibility*

> 12 WHEREFORE, MY BELOVED, AS YE HAVE ALWAYS OBEYED, NOT AS IN MY PRESENCE ONLY, BUT NOW MUCH MORE IN MY ABSENCE, **WORK OUT YOUR OWN SALVATION WITH FEAR AND TREMBLING. KJV**

A Testimony

For five years, I never went up on that prayer line without saying to God, what do you want me to get delivered from? What do I have to do to get that deliverance? And God never failed to answer my prayer. *Work out your own salvation* means find out how God intends to deliver you, and go and do what he requires of you, no matter how much it hurts. If you can just get this vision, it is easy.

Do not worry about your feelings. Just find out what is right, and do it. This revelation will save our lives. Do not follow your emotions, because living out of your emotions is the scriptural definition of *spiritual death*. Find out from God what is right in a given situation, and do it. Forget about your pride. Do not worry about what you may lose, just do what God tells you to do and you cannot fail. Do not live out of your emotions, which are easily manipulated by the carnal mind.

Sanctification & Truth?

2 Thes 2:13 - *Sanctification*

> 13 BUT WE ARE BOUND TO GIVE THANKS ALWAYS TO GOD FOR YOU, BRETHREN BELOVED OF THE LORD, BECAUSE **GOD HATH CHOSEN YOU TO SALVATION, THROUGH SANCTIFICATION OF THE SPIRIT AND BELIEF OF THE TRUTH. KJV**

Sanctification separates the thoughts of our mind, and helps us to distinguish between what is right and what is wrong.

Truth Is The Spirit Of Christ

<u>John 14:17</u> *– Spirit of Truth*

17 EVEN **THE SPIRIT OF TRUTH; WHOM THE WORLD CANNOT RECEIVE,** BECAUSE IT SEETH HIM NOT, NEITHER KNOWETH HIM: BUT YE KNOW HIM; FOR HE DWELLETH WITH YOU, AND SHALL BE IN YOU. **KJV**

The Holy Spirit is the Spirit of Promise . . .

<u>Eph 1:13</u> *– Spirit of Promise*

13 IN WHOM YE ALSO TRUSTED, AFTER THAT YE HEARD THE WORD OF TRUTH, THE GOSPEL OF YOUR SALVATION: IN WHOM ALSO AFTER THAT YE BELIEVED, **YE WERE SEALED WITH THAT HOLY SPIRIT OF PROMISE,** **KJV**

but it is not the Spirit of Truth. We experience the Spirit of Truth when we recognize and resist the thoughts of our carnal mind.

Wisdom?

<u>2 Tim 3:15</u> *– Salvation Through Faith*

15 AND THAT FROM A CHILD THOU HAST KNOWN THE HOLY SCRIPTURES, WHICH ARE ABLE TO MAKE THEE WISE UNTO **SALVATION THROUGH FAITH WHICH IS IN CHRIST JESUS. KJV**

<u>2 Tim 3:15</u> *- Wise Unto Salvation*

15 AND THAT FROM A CHILD THOU HAST KNOWN **THE HOLY SCRIPTURES,** WHICH ARE ABLE TO **MAKE THEE WISE UNTO SALVATION** THROUGH FAITH WHICH IS IN CHRIST JESUS. **KJV**

Read the Scriptures. Learn the Scriptures. Read the Law of God. All of the Scripture is good, but brethren learn the Law of God. It will make you *wise unto salvation*.

We need more than the power to cast out demons. We need wisdom to help suffering people stop bringing destruction upon themselves. God is bringing us to a place where we can reveal why people have problems in their lives, and why they are birthing demons, to help them move into a full *Salvation of their soul*.

An Anchor?

Heb 6:19 – *Jesus, Our Anchor*

19 WHICH HOPE WE HAVE AS **AN ANCHOR OF THE SOUL**, BOTH SURE AND STEDFAST, AND WHICH ENTERETH INTO THAT WITHIN THE VEIL. **KJV**

What is Jesus anchoring us to? He is anchoring us to the spiritual realm of God. All provision, life, safety, peace and happiness, are through the power of the spiritual realm of God, as revealed in the Garden of Eden.

Joel 2:3 – *Garden Of Eden*

3 A FIRE DEVOURETH BEFORE THEM; AND BEHIND THEM A FLAME BURNETH: THE LAND IS AS THE GARDEN OF EDEN BEFORE THEM, AND BEHIND THEM A DESOLATE WILDERNESS; YEA, AND NOTHING SHALL ESCAPE THEM. **KJV**

Not only are we going back to Eden, we will be anchored there, never to be separated from God again. We will experience God's total provision. But when we experience the immortality of innocence the second time, we will have memories of our seduction and overcoming experiences with evil, and will appreciate what we have. This is just a fact of life, brethren. People do not appreciate what they have until they lose it.

Today?

2 Cor 6:2 – *Salvation Today*

> 2 (FOR HE SAITH, I HAVE HEARD THEE IN A TIME
> ACCEPTED, AND IN THE DAY OF SALVATION HAVE I
> SUCCOURED THEE: BEHOLD, NOW IS THE ACCEPTED TIME;
> BEHOLD, **NOW IS THE DAY OF SALVATION.**) **KJV**

What does *today is the day of salvation*, mean? There are millions of people out there in the world that are not saved. What does *today* mean? What is *today*? *Today* is an age.

When we receive the promise, God lays hold of us and something spiritual happens inside of us. We move into another age called *the day of salvation*.

An Age?

Eph 3:21 – *World Without End*

> 21 UNTO HIM BE GLORY IN THE CHURCH BY CHRIST
> JESUS THROUGHOUT ALL AGES, **WORLD WITHOUT END.**
> AMEN. **KJV**

The New Age that everybody is waiting for, is Jesus Christ. When we move into this realm, the New Age is in our heart. It starts as a mustard seed, and it grow up and fills our entire being. We become a New Age Man. A New Creation Man comes forth from within us, not from outside of us.

Forever?

Ps 89:36 – *Salvation For All Time*

> 36 HIS SEED SHALL ENDURE FOREVER, AND HIS
> THRONE AS THE SUN BEFORE ME. **KJV**

Isa 51:8 – *No More Aging*

> 8 FOR THE MOTH SHALL EAT THEM UP LIKE A
> GARMENT, AND THE WORM SHALL EAT THEM LIKE WOOL: BUT
> MY RIGHTEOUSNESS SHALL BE FOR EVER, AND **MY SALVATION
> FROM GENERATION TO GENERATION. KJV**

We will stop aging after our soul is saved and our body is adopted. Eye has not seen and ear has not heard, what God has in store for us. But we know that exciting experiences are waiting for us!

Eccl 3:11 – *Ages In The Heart*

> 11 HE HATH MADE EVERY THING BEAUTIFUL IN HIS
> TIME: ALSO **HE HATH SET THE [AGES] IN THEIR HEART,** SO
> THAT NO MAN CAN FIND OUT THE WORK THAT GOD MAKETH
> FROM THE BEGINNING TO THE END. **KJV**

The ages are within us, in our heart. We are going from age to age. Most of us here are in the age of perfection. That age is within us. It has nothing to do with August 1988. We exist in the age of perfection because we partake of the experiences of that age.

The next age that is coming is ***glorification***. We get there by staying right where we are in this world. If it is the timetable of God and He wills to do it, we could wake up tomorrow morning in the age of glorification, because something happened to our heart, not because we moved to any natural, carnal place.

We do not know which age comes after the age of glorification, but the Bible says something about two thousand generations, two thousand ages. We do not know what God will be doing in those ages, but we know that it will be glorious.

Being in the age of perfection does not mean that we are perfect, but that you are a candidate to become perfect. We have to exist in a realm where perfection is possible, if we are to experience it. Perfection is the perfection of our soul, which means that our soul will be made sinless.

First, our soul must become subject to the Spirit of Holiness through Christ Jesus, who is joining His spotless soul to our soul. No one is sinless yet, except Jesus, The Church is moving into that experience.

To get to the point of **Perfection**, we have to be in a place where it is available. If we want to eat, we have to come into the kitchen. We cannot be out in the garden and expect the food to come to us. Perfection comes to us, through Christ Jesus, within us. As He grows and matures within us, all the promises of God become available to us, according to the spiritual maturity of the Christ within you.

It is the body that is glorified. Our dead body cannot be glorified when our soul is elsewhere. If we exist in an age where glorification is not yet available, which is today, and our body corrupts, our soul must receive another body when our turn comes for glorification.

We must have a body and a soul that are attached to each other to be made incorruptible.

There is a lot of speculation about how people will get their spiritual bodies. Some believe that their original body that they lived in the earth will be glorified, but that is not likely.

Eccl 12:7 – *Dust To Dust*

> 7 THEN SHALL THE DUST RETURN TO THE EARTH
> AS IT WAS: AND THE SPIRIT SHALL RETURN UNTO GOD WHO
> GAVE IT   **KJV**

The spirit and soul of a man have a body formed from the substance of the world that the mind dwells in. An ascended mind acquires an ascended body, and the physical body returns to the dust of this spiritually low visible plane of existence.

<u>1 Tim 6:14-16</u> - *Immortality Only Through Jesus*

14 . . . UNTIL THE APPEARING OF **OUR LORD JESUS CHRIST:**

15 WHICH IN HIS TIMES HE SHALL SHEW, WHO IS THE BLESSED AND **ONLY POTENTATE**, THE KING OF KINGS, AND LORD OF LORDS;

16 **WHO ONLY HATH IMMORTALITY**, DWELLING IN THE LIGHT WHICH NO MAN CAN APPROACH UNTO; WHOM NO MAN HATH SEEN, NOR CAN SEE: TO WHOM BE HONOUR AND POWER EVERLASTING. AMEN. **KJV**

Jesus Christ is the *Savior* of our soul and a *Redeemer* of our spirit. He is our potential to join with the father, the only source of true immortality

.

TABLE OF REFERENCES

ABOUT THE AUTHOR

Sheila R. Vitale is the Spiritual Leader, Founding Teacher, and Pastor of *Living Epistles Ministries (LEM)*. She moves in the offices of Teacher of Apostolic Doctrine, Prophet, Evangelist and Pastor, has an international following, and has been expounding on the Scripture through a unique spiritual lens for nearly three decades.

She has written more than 50 books based on the Old and New Testaments including *Ephraim, Man of the Earth* and *The Eagle Ascended (OT),* and *Salvation* and *Not Without Blood (NT).* She has also rendered original spiritual interpretations of Biblical texts such as *The Woman in The Well (John, Chapter 4)* and *First Corinthians, Chapter 11.* Her unique, Multi-Part Message style is seen in *LEM* Serial Messages such as *A Place Teeming With Life* (9 Parts) and *Quantum Mechanics in Creation* (18 Parts). Each Part of a Multi-Part Message Series can also be enjoyed as a complete and independent study. In addition, she has defined, explained, illustrated and demonstrated hundreds of spiritual principles throughout more than 1,000 *LEM* Lectures.

Her signature work, however, is the three volumes of *The Alternate Translation Bible (ATB)*: *The Alternate Translation of The Old Testament, The Alternate Translation of The New Testament* and *The Alternate Translation of the Book of Revelation. The Alternate Translation Bible* is a work in progress (*The ATB Project*). Accordingly, additional spiritual interpretations of both whole and partial Chapters are added from time to time, as they are rendered. The most up-to-date versions of *The ATB Project* may be found online at *The LEM* W*ebsite* (*LivingEpistles.org*). *The ATB* is a *spiritual interpretation* of the Scripture and is not intended to replace traditional translations.

She also analyzed the Greek text of *The Book of Revelation* and preached extensively on it in the early years of *The ATB Project*. During that time she produced 197 distinct *Message Parts*, under 29 specific *Message Titles*, all of which deal with *The Book of Revelation*. Also, many of her books such as, *Adam and The Two Judgments* and *A Study in Unconscious Mind Control*, have been translated into Spanish, as well as *The Book of Revelation*.

Pastor Vitale is an illustrator of spiritual principles, a researcher, a translator and a reviewer of the Modern Social Trends of Family and Culture, as they are revealed through TV programs (*The Sopranos),* movies (*The Matrix* and *The Edge of Tomorrow)* and plays (*Wicked).* She also writes for the *LEM Blog.*

She travels domestically, as well as internationally, preaching and teaching Judeo-Christian Spiritual Philosophy, and has donated Audio Libraries of her Lectures to other ministries in Africa, Asia, Europe and North America,

Pastor Vitale serves *LEM* in a range of spiritual, educational, and administrative functions from *The Selden Centre, LEM* headquarters in Selden, New York. She is also a philanthropic individual who supports the *Lighthouse Mission (Patchogue, NY) and HGM – Mission of Hope – Haiti, and other* charitable organizations. She also supports community services such as the *Terryville Fire Department.*

In her spare time, Pastor Vitale enjoys watching movies, attending plays and partaking of cuisines from different cultures. An avid traveler, she has visited several countries in Europe and Africa as well as many cities in the United States.

BEGINNINGS, INSPIRATION AND CALLING

Pastor Vitale began her spiritual journey as a child when her Jewish mother enrolled her in the Hebrew school of an Orthodox synagogue. She experienced the Spirit of God for the first time there in such a profound way that she wept. But after that, when she was only eleven years old, she became very ill and was taken to Mount Sinai Hospital in New York City. She almost died there and has battled with life-threatening health issues ever since. Nevertheless, a deep longing for God continued to pursue her until several years later when she desperately wanted to attend Yeshiva (Jewish high school), but could not. Her secular parents approved of her choice, but could not afford the tuition.

Much later, after years of searching, she once again experienced the Spirit that had brought her to tears in the synagogue of her youth, but this time it was at *Gospel Revivals Ministries*, a Pentecostal church where Deliverance Ministry was emphasized. She had a desire to understand the Bible since she was a child, but Scripture was difficult for her and she struggled with the text. Nevertheless, she read one Chapter of the Bible every day until, one day, *her spiritual eyes opened* and she saw an angel holding a little book.

After that, she attended as many as five teaching services each week for about seven years, the latter part of which she edited *Pastor Holzhauser's* books. But several more years had to pass before *the eyes of her understanding opened even further* and she began to receive *Revelation Knowledge of the Scripture*. She understood at that time that the angel she had seen was the angel of Revelation 10:8.

After about seven years of learning *Deliverance Ministry* and *The Doctrine of Sonship* (*Bill Britton*) from *Pastor Holzhauser,* she studied the Bible independently under the influence and direction of the Holy Spirit.

In **1998** she began teaching Apostolic Doctrine.

In **1990** she spent three months in Stony Brook Hospital where she recovered from an incurable disease, defeating premature death, once again, and went on to resume teaching and managing *LEM.*

In **1992** she journeyed to Africa for the first time, where she was called to the office of Evangelist.

In the **mid-1990s,** she began to Pastor in addition to being a Teacher of Apostolic Doctrine, a Prophet and an Evangelist, thus, satisfying all five offices of *The Ministry of the Lord Jesus Christ to His Church.*

LIVING EPISTLES MINISTRIES

Pastor Vitale was happy fellowshipping at *Gospel Revivals Ministries* but, eventually, she desired a deeper and more spiritual understanding of the Word of God. One day, after crying out to Jesus about her need, she was amazed to hear Him ask her if she would teach. Her initial response was that she did not see how it would be possible since she was already working a full-time job, despite her poor health. But after the Lord asked her for a second and then a third time, she reluctantly agreed, believing that He would empower her to do the job. Shortly thereafter, in the latter part of 1987, she began to teach her own brand of Judeo-Christian Spiritual Philosophy.

The Lord Jesus Christ named the work *Living Epistles Ministries* in 1988.

The first *LEM* meetings were casual and spontaneous gatherings of friends and fellow deliverance workers in Pastor

Vitale's home. After that, they were held in the business office of one of the brethren. Pastor Vitale delivered her first formal message entitled *The Truth About Witchcraft in January of 1988*, followed by *The Seduction of Eve* in April of the same year. After that, she prepared and taught weekly messages including *Signs of Apostleship* and *Lazarus & The Rich Man*. The meetings eventually increased to two and then three each week.

Sometime after that, she learned that the Lord Jesus Christ was revealing spiritual principles from the Hebrew text of the Old Testament through her teachings, and she used those spiritual principles to begin to unlock the mysteries of the New Testament, as well. Today she understands that the Scripture is a spiritual document that must be spiritually discerned if it is to be understood correctly, and calls that spiritual understanding **The Doctrine of Christ**.

LEM publishes a wide range of material, including books, e-books, spiritual interpretations of the Scripture and transcripts of many of Pastor Vitale's Lectures and on-line meetings, all of which, as well as the entire *Alternate Translation Bible,* may be viewed free of charge on the *LEM* website (*LivingEpistles.org*). She also has an *Author's Website* where all of her books, as well as several photographs of herself and a short biography are displayed (Amazon.com/author/SheilaVitale). Paperback and digital versions of *LEM* books may be purchased through *Amazon, Google Books* and *Barnes & Noble*.

LEM provides free video livestreams through YouTube and other Internet Platforms . . .

@LivingEpistlesMinistries (2016 – Sept. 2022)
@LivingEpistlesMinistriesLEM ((Oct. 2022 – Ongoing)
@LivingEpistlesMinistries (LEM disciples)

. . . as well as two channels of **Shortclips** where short, focused messages of about 15 minutes each are posted:

@shortclipsbysheilar.vitale3334 (2016 – Sept. 2022)
@ShortClips-SheilaVitale (Oct. 2022 – Ongoing)

LEM donates a significant percentage of its income to other Christian ministries and organizations that advocate for Christian values and defend the United States Constitution.

PASTOR VITALE TODAY

Today Pastor Vitale continues to dedicate her life to teaching the spiritual principles of the Bible and focuses daily on studying, writing and preaching powerful messages from *The Selden Centre,* LEM/CCK's headquarters at Selden, New York.

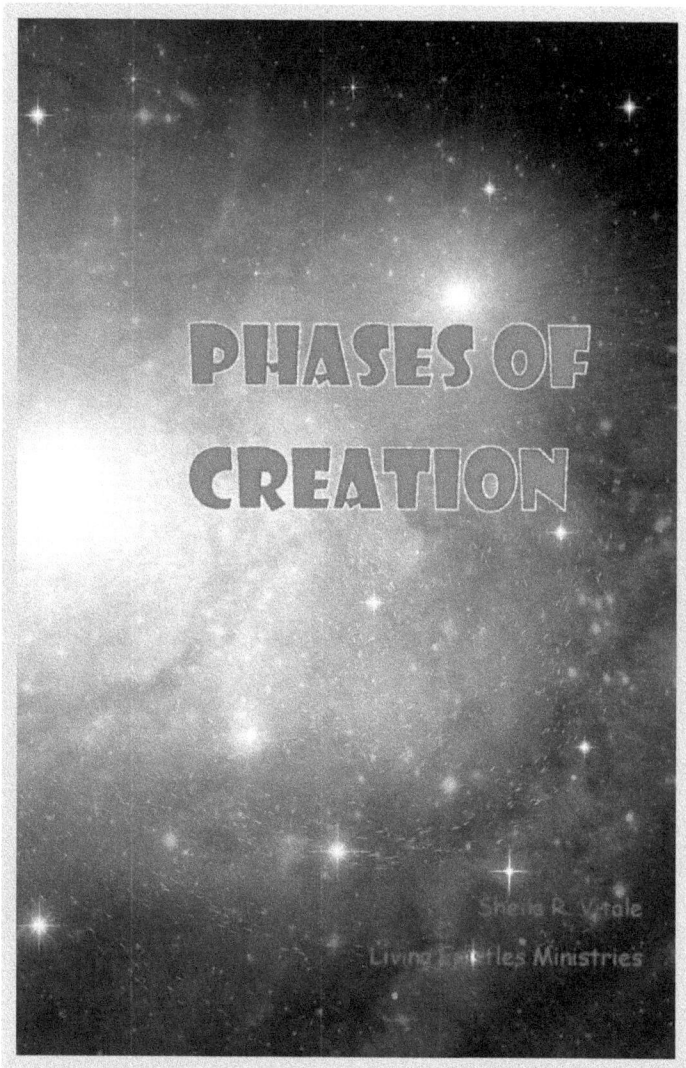

Phases of Creation has two distinct sections. The first Section is an esoteric treatise on creation. The second Section deals with deception in the Church

THE TRUTH ABOUT BAPTISM

A Study in Baptism & Tongues

Sheila R. Vitale
Living Epistles Ministries

The Truth About Baptism is a study in Baptism and Tongues. Subtopics include, Prophecy, The Gospel of the Cross vs. the Gospel of Perfection, and the Spirit of Antichrist

NOT WITHOUT BLOOD

Understanding The New Covenant
2nd Edition

Sheila R. Vitale
Living Epistles Ministries

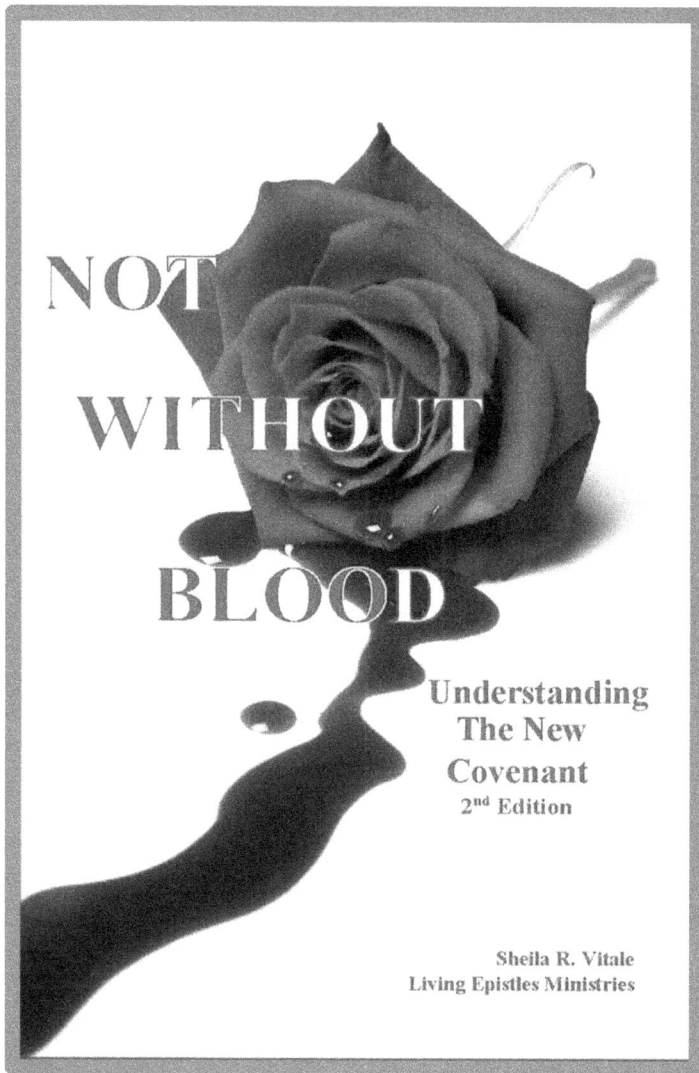

Not Without Blood explains that Jesus' sacrifice gained access to the throne of God for all mankind, but that each individual must offer up his own sin nature in exchange for Jesus' righteousness nature.

Living Epistles Ministries
Judeo-Christian Spiritual Philosophy
Sheila R. Vitale
Pastor, Teacher & Founder
PO Box 562, Port Jefferson Station, New York 11776, USA
LivingEpistles.org
or
Books@LivingEpistles.org

www.ingramcontent.com/pod-product-compliance
Lightning Source LLC
Chambersburg PA
CBHW072200090426
42740CB00012B/2335